Before It Was Legal

a black-white marriage (1945-1987)

Before It Was Legal:
a black-white marriage (1945-1987)

Nancy Werking Poling

Screech Owl Press

Published by:
Screech Owl Press
624 Azalea Ave.
Black Mountain, NC 28711

www.NancyPoling.com

In conjunction with:
Old Mountain Press, Inc.
85 John Allman Ln.
Sylva, NC 28779

www.OldMountainPress.com
Old Mountain Press eBook Division
www.oldmp.com/e-book

First Edition
10 9 8 7 6 5 4 3 2 1

Also by Nancy Werking Poling

Had Eve Come First and Jonah Been a Woman
a collection of short stories in which heroes of Hebrew
Scripture are imagined as women.

Out of the Pumpkin Shell
a novel about women's friendship and family secrets.

Victim to Survivor: women recovering from clergy sexual abuse
Nancy Werking Poling, editor.

In memory of Anna and Daniel

Acknowledgments

M Y THANKS TO those who offered information and advice in this project:

The Earlham College Library;

Carol Werking LaRue, my cousin, who loaned me her mother's (Violet's) diaries;

Carl Henderson, Daniel's friend and coworker at International Harvester;

Inez Long, deceased, Anna's college roommate;

Paul Robinson, deceased, nephew of Anna's father's second wife;

My husband, Jim Poling, who never stops encouraging me to tell the stories.

Preface

IN AUGUST, 1986, I traveled to Mexico City in search of a love story. Anna, a white woman, was my aunt's sister. She and Daniel, an African American, gave up family, friends, even country, to spend a lifetime together. Their marriage, illegal in Indiana during the 1940s and as long as they lived there, was accepted in Mexico.

I went to Mexico assuming theirs was a narrative about a man and woman whose love overcame society's limitations, who in their later years were living out the *happily ever after.* Not until our last day together, a result of the trust that had grown between us, did they tell me what they had originally not intended to speak of. So while there is no *happily ever after,* what follows is an honest portrayal of a marriage, of its hurt and anger. It is also a story of how at the end of their lives a couple tried to make sense of their relationship.

In our eleven days together the two of them shared much more than the story of their marriage; they shared their home and friendship. I shall always feel privileged for having had the opportunity to know them. Daniel died of a heart attack five months after our time together. Anna has also died since then.

RELYING ON FIRST-PERSON accounts has potential pitfalls. The go-between writer must decide when to trust the narrators' memories—which, in this case, extended back even further than World War I—and their interpretation of events. When I could, I checked facts, but that was not always possible. Sometimes, deciding it would not hurt if the name of a street or person was incorrect, I chose to leave it in. For example, when Daniel told of his initial encounters with union organizers, he mentioned Jack Carpenter from Chicago, a man whose identity I was unable to confirm. I left the name in. At other times I made the opposite decision.

Daniel was a masterful story teller, able to include the kinds of details that made his past fascinating. Accounts of his experiences often approach verbatim. Anna, however, tended to describe an event in three or four sentences, telling more about how she felt than about the setting or other people. To make their individual pasts equally interesting I have brought my imagination into the narrative, adding dialogue and plausible descriptions.

I have also added a historical strand, for the people we become, the decisions we make occur within a historical context. Sometimes we make choices that are in harmony with our culture; sometimes we choose to go against it. Wanting the reader to understand how radical Anna's and Daniel's decision to marry was for that era, I have told about historical events—all of which occurred during their lifetimes—mainly on the basis of the events' pertinence to white attitudes toward African Americans in general and toward interracial marriage in particular. There's no way for us to know the extent to which Daniel and Anna were knowledgeable about these incidents, though it is likely that Daniel was very aware.

Another strand, the beginning of each chapter, follows Anna's possible thoughts during the interview process. While another's mind is inaccessible, I know now what I did not know until the last day of the interview: how the story ended. I have imagined what Anna must have been thinking all along.

One other note: Daniel preferred the term *Negro* to *black* or *African American*. I use all three terms but try to stay true to his choice of words and to the historical period.

For reasons that will become obvious, I have changed their names and the names of living relatives.

Chapter 1

A S IF BLIND, she moves her fingers across the familiar surface of the ring. Two profiles, one black, one white, carved on onyx; January 25, 1941, engraved inside the band. The evening Daniel invited her to watch him teach his WPA class. "It was snowing," she used to write on scraps of paper, little reminders about that night, that kiss. Left on his pillow or beside his plate at breakfast.

She remembers when he quit wearing the ring, her wedding gift to him. He brushed off her dismay, said something about it symbolizing the early days of their marriage, before they moved to Mexico. But it's that earlier love she'll hold, the love she wants her daughters and their children to remember.

In an almost supernatural way she feels his presence with her now, here in the alcove between living room and kitchen. Above the desk hang his framed diplomas from Earlham and his master's program, the picture of the girls and her taken at a studio while he was studying down here, the retirement citation presented by the school where he taught English for twenty-five years.

Letters, newspaper articles, photos he collected all those years, his existence on this planet chronicled in his desk and file cabinet. How many hours he spent in here after retirement, leafing through his lifetime. How many treks upstairs to show her an article featuring him in the *Chicago Defender* or to tell her the story behind a photo he came across.

She thumbs through the file containing his collection of newspaper clippings about black athletes: Jessie Owens at the Berlin Olympics, Satchel Paige, the Brown Bomber. An outstanding athlete himself, he never was able to understand a man who didn't like sports.

Another folder: mementoes from their courtship and early days of their marriage. Letters she wrote after her transfer to northern Indiana. A ticket stub for *Meet me in St. Louis,* shown at the movie theater where they used to sit in the colored balcony. The carbon copy of a love poem he wrote for her. Maybe she'll combine his collection with her own, pass it all on to the girls.

His union file, thickest of them all. Harvester hired him as a janitor, didn't think Negro men were intelligent enough to operate machinery. But the union saw use for his education.

Then she notices it. In the back of the drawer, an envelope addressed to him. She recognizes the feminine handwriting. Knives lodge in her heart, wrenched back and forth by an invisible hand. She whimpers. But she'll not open the envelope. She refrained from snooping when he was alive; she'll not start now.

She takes comfort knowing that this time he did not leave her of his own accord.

Chapter 2

*H*OW OFTEN SHE'S *seen him this way: long legs crossed, erect posture giving him an air of dignity. From the beginning she was attracted by the glimmer and intensity of his dark eyes. They still affect her.*

They sit on opposite ends of the sofa, a tape recorder in between. Though Daniel uses inflection or a dramatic tone for authoritative affect, his voice is usually subdued, as if he has something worthwhile to say and it would be to the listener's advantage to pay careful attention. It is that ability to speak quietly and still be forceful that helped him succeed in his union years. And it's what made him a good teacher.

He uses his hands as he speaks, not in an excessively demonstrative way, but in a manner as controlled and as deliberate as his speech. Such hands—slender, graceful hands that seem custom-made for basketballs and tennis rackets he gripped through much of his life. Sensuous hands that have stroked her hair, caressed her body.

As usual, his appearance is meticulous. When not in a hurry herself, she's watched him carefully inspect his attire in the mirror, his long, agile fingers removing a piece of lint, positioning the shirt collar, making certain a crease is where it should be.

Now she listens as he again makes it clear that a white woman can never understand what it was like for a Negro boy to grow to manhood during the 1920s.

IMMEDIATELY AFTER THE Civil War ended his status as a slave, Daniel's great-grandfather, a young man of twenty-four, stopped at Richmond, Indiana, en route to the West. When someone offered him a job shoveling coal at the foundry, he stayed and built a crude hut on a vacant lot at the edge of town. Eventually he took a wife: the granddaughter of a French trader and a Cherokee Indian.

Daniel's mother, Pearl, was eighteen in 1908, when he was born. The child's father, a thirty-seven-year-old man, wanted to marry her, but her father opposed the marriage. Supposedly she complied with his wishes, though it's hard to imagine headstrong Pearl giving in to pressure from anyone. She named her son after her father: Daniel Winters. Friends and relatives made it clear they doubted she could raise a boy on her own. She made it clear that she indeed could and embarked on parenthood determined to single-handedly shape the child into a well-behaved and responsible man.

Tall and slender, Pearl was an attractive woman with skin the color of a robin's breast. At the end of the day, no matter how many hours she'd spent as a cleaning lady at Richmond's hospital, she accompanied her home chores with the soprano melodies she sang in the church choir. A studio portrait of Daniel and his mother shows her standing against a small table, her mid-calf skirt covering most of her buttoned boots. Beside her little Daniel holds a stick that turns a small wheel. He wears a sailor suit with short pants. His head of long, curly hair makes him appear more like a girl than a boy.

Grandpa Winters lived with Pearl and her son. Maybe because they were both frequently the objects of Pearl's wrath, the two males of the household developed a special bond. When Daniel knew his mother was about to whip him, he'd run to his grandfather for refuge. Seated in a large overstuffed chair, Grandpa reached toward Daniel, wrapped his long arms and legs around the boy, and placed his shoulders in a protective posture, an act that seldom failed to increase Pearl's fury.

It wasn't unusual back then for little boys to wear their hair long. Pearl had been letting Daniel's hair grow, fixing it in curls, braids, or wrapped around his head and held in place by hairpins. One day Grandpa, without saying a word, took his three-year-old grandson to the barber.

"I want this boy to *look* like a boy," he said.

Daniel howled as he watched his long black curls fall to the floor. What he saw in the mirror made him cry harder: a boy wearing his clothes, tears running down his face, with practically no hair at all.

A piece of candy in his mouth and a curl wrapped in a piece of paper sufficiently pacified him so that when he walked in the door of his house he could smile at his mother. But one look at her shorn son brought on an explosion. Daniel was her son. She would decide when he was to get a haircut.

The long, bulky skirt and cumbersome shoes would have slowed a less determined woman tearing a path to the barbershop. Held tightly by the wrist Daniel had no choice but to run alongside his mother as fast as his legs would carry him.

"Mr. Hyatt." Her sudden confrontational entry startled barber and customers. Still grasping Daniel's wrist she pointed at his head with her free hand. "As long as I live, don't you ever cut my boy's hair without my permission."

Mr. Hyatt answered as even the toughest of men would have: "Yes, ma'am."

Not until Daniel was eight did Pearl take him back for a haircut. Even when as a young adult he went to Mr. Hyatt's barbershop, the barber asked, "Are you sure this is the way your mother wants your hair cut?"

RICHMOND, INDIANA, WHERE Daniel spent nearly all of his first forty-nine years, is located near the Ohio state line. Preeminent among the area's early settlers were Friends whose opposition to slavery led them to leave their homes in the South. Over the decades the Quakers' social conscience had a strong influence on the community. Many a runaway slave, assisted by Friends, intended to pass through Richmond en route to Canada or to the West but ended up a permanent resident. The quarries and mills needed laborers accustomed to hard physical work.

Quaker presence impacted the community's support and commitment to education. In the mid-1800s the Yearly Meeting opened a boarding school for Quaker secondary students. In 1859 it became Earlham College, which later enjoyed a national reputation for academic excellence and a local reputation for liberal, hence, according to some residents, *unpatriotic,* politics.

Situated at the confluence of river and railroad, resting on vast deposits of stone and gravel, Richmond was able to develop a firm industrial base. In the mid-1800s construction of the National Road, which became for many years the most heavily traveled highway in the country, brought scores of immigrant laborers, mainly from Germany, to the area. Eventually they brought their families and stayed. Over the years, as they became insiders—owners of mortuaries, department stores, and factories—this group fell into a conservative mindset.

In spite of the strong Quaker influence, Richmond was as segregated as cities of the South. Restaurants, ice cream parlors, beaches, and hotels were all off-limits to the city's black population. While they were allowed to attend the three local movie theaters, they had to sit in the balcony. Only one restaurant, down by the factories, served them. Its owner, operator, cook, waitress, and dishwasher was a small-framed black woman with a phenomenal metabolic rate and down-home culinary abilities that made the toughest of men homesick for Mama's cooking.

As delicious as the proprietor's fatback and greens were, hers was not a place for special occasions. There were no restaurants where a black man could wine and dine the woman he loved; none where his family could celebrate a birthday meal; none where he and his friends could meet for a special dinner. Neither were African-American celebrities allowed to spend the night in any of Richmond's hotels. A middle-aged widow had a few extra rooms, which she rented to well-known personalities such as Louis Armstrong, Joe Lewis, and Marianne Anderson.

Denied participation in the life of the wider community, Richmond's African Americans developed their own social networks. Negro Elks and Masons built meeting halls, which they rented to other groups for eleven dollars a night. The Esquires, a social club organized by a group of young men, frequently rented a hall for a big party. Since all the caterers in town were white, the Esquires' dates had to prepare and bring the food.

The Winters's home was on the town's north side, where mainly Negroes and immigrants lived. It was a community of neighborliness, with everybody looking out for everybody else. If one family suffered from an illness or accident, neighbors brought in covered dishes and helped take care of the children. An Italian or German or Jewish family, when it became more affluent, would move to another part of town, but a black family had to stay on the north side.

A PRECOCIOUS CHILD, Daniel skipped half a year in second grade, then another half year at the end of third. He always lived in fear, however, that the principal would send him back a grade for an infraction of a rule, such as whispering in class, since he was by nature a gregarious child.

When he wasn't in school or doing chores, he was organizing sports activities. It wasn't uncommon for five or six boys to set up a boxing match, each contributing what he could to the effort. Thaddeus always insisted that since one of the pairs of boxing gloves was his, he should be referee. Herman, who had taken his father's watch off the bureau, was in charge of making sure rounds lasted three minutes. When a round came to an end, the competitors rested. There weren't many rules, except low punches weren't allowed.

If other boys couldn't come out to play, Daniel would dunk a stuffed sock through a cardboard carton he'd nailed to the side of the house. Pretending there were two teams, he'd spend hours shooting baskets, first as a player on one team, then on the other. He'd keep score and when his mother called him in—he never quit from being tired—the team with the most points was declared the winner. No matter who won, he was jubilant.

But he could only play after he'd finished household chores, which his mother made sure he did painstakingly. Many a summer evening, after he'd completed—or *thought* he'd completed—his chores, he'd be absorbed in a game of mumble peg, about to flip the knife over his shoulder, when his mother's voice would carry throughout the neighborhood: "Daaa-nyulll!" (People in the church choir complained that Pearl's voice drowned out all the others.)

"Ma'am?" he called out, trying to sound innocent, though he knew it wouldn't work. (*Yes, ma'am, no ma'am,* he didn't dare say anything else.)

"You come back in the kitchen and do your job right."

No short-cut went undetected. Not only would he have to rewash the glass that was streaked; he had to rewash all the glasses. He scrubbed the stove top under his mother's watchful eye. He re-swept the floor, making certain that every particle of dust went into the dustpan.

Daniel: "So I learned that when I finished the kitchen, I had to check. I checked the stove to see if there was any grease on it. I checked the dishes. Everything. I knew that if I did it well and went out to play, there was no problem. To this day I have an antipathy for circuses. In those days the circus came to town three of four times in the summer. They sold little whips. My mother would buy those whips, and between the dog and me, she'd wear them out. In my mind a circus still mean whips."

He had just turned eight when he started going to dances with Pearl. At first he sat on a chair alongside the dance floor, carefully watching as couples glided, dipped, and swirled by. Later at home he danced through the house with a broom, thinking that would help him know what it was like to hold on to someone. At nine he became his mother's primary dance partner, a practice that continued into his junior high years.

Daniel: "My relationship with her was certainly complex. She was strict, but I never thought of her as mean. While she was hard on me, she also delighted in my presence and accomplishments. One thing she gave me, that a lifetime of racial prejudice could never take away—that was a feeling of pride. I don't say this often, because it sounds egotistical, but because of my mother I grew up knowing I was a very special person. Not that I am better than others, but at age seventy-eight I still believe that I'm special."

KAISER. VICTORY GARDEN. Western Front. Daniel didn't understand the words; he only knew that The War in Europe, later known as World War I, gave him social status. As captain of his school's gardening project—where each student was responsible for a six-by-six-foot plot at the end of the baseball diamond—he got to wear a badge.

Not that he was unaware of American men fighting in Europe. Sometimes he accompanied his mother to the train station, where she assisted the Negro women's auxiliary in giving cigarettes to the cars of Negro soldiers passing through town.

On the night of November 11, 1918, a Richmond man kept vigil so he could alert the town when official word announced the war's end. The announcement came in the middle of the night; festivities started at daybreak.

Everything halted for the celebration. Factories shut down, schools closed. Country folks came into town, and people mingled freely, age and race making no difference. Noise, Daniel had never heard such a commotion. Factory whistles blared; church bells rang; men shot pistols and shotguns in the air. Hundreds of cars pulled tin cans, garbage barrels, wash boilers, anything that would make a racket. A group of women carrying alarm clocks formed a procession, and there were mini-parades of people hitting metal dishpans, pie tins, and skillets.

He was standing beside Pearl, who was pounding on her dishpan with a wooden spoon, when a large flat-bed truck stopped and the driver yelled, "To hell with the Kaiser. Come on boys, get in." Not bothering to check with his mother, Daniel jumped on and rode up and down the street several times.

At about eleven o'clock that night, holding his mother's hand and leaning against her, he walked back to their house on North Fifteenth Street.

ON A SUNDAY morning in January, dressed in their Sunday best, mother and son were about to go out the front door when Pearl announced that from then on they would attend the Bethel AME Church. Keeping about three paces in front of Daniel, she took rapid, deliberate steps in the direction opposite the one leading to the Baptist Church she'd attended all her life. She never admitted it, but word spread at the Baptist Church that she wanted to have the best voice in the choir, and she didn't like taking a backseat to her niece, Carrie.

Carrie had recently returned from two years of studying voice in Rome. She came home with talent and hope but no audience. The few who could afford to attend performances were white people unwilling to listen to a woman of color sing. Those who enjoyed her music, the town's black population, didn't have any money. So she married a custodian at the hospital and shared her talent with members of the Baptist Church.

Organized in 1836, the Bethel AME Church was located on the site of an old blacksmith shop. Today it is recognized as the oldest black congregation in Indiana. In about 1920, when the congregation built an addition onto the original church building, workers unearthed the smithy's scraps and mistakes. Fascinated by artifacts that gave evidence of the land's prior use, every member's daughter or son, including Daniel, had a collection of rusty nails and pieces of iron. The men of the church built the addition themselves. Weary from their day's work, nearly always at a job requiring physical labor, they came every summer evening and stayed until darkness made work impossible. In November the addition was completed and dedicated.

WHEN HER FATHER died, Pearl married Clifford Thurman, a car mechanic. Daniel hated him. Although Pearl ordered Thurman never to lay a hand on her boy—she alone had that right and duty—he ignored her instructions whenever he was home alone with his step-son.

One morning, after his mother had gone to work, Daniel came down from his room, ready for school. From the kitchen Thurman's churlish voice demanded, "You, Daniel, come here." Ignoring him, Daniel walked to the table in the living room to get his books.

"When I tell you—" Thurman entered the room, his arm extended, palm open. In one smooth movement Daniel headed toward the sofa and reached behind it for a board he'd hidden there for such an occasion. He leaped on the sofa arm, and at the moment Thurman drew back his hand, Daniel began pounding with all his might on Thurman's head. Even with the added height and the weapon the boy was no match for an adult man. Thurman seized the board and threw it across the room before he grabbed Daniel, flung him on the floor, and kicked him.

Daniel: "He was always mean to me. One time I threw a jar of cold cream at him. I can still see it missing him, hitting the wall, and breaking into pieces. For Christmas they bought me a single shot .22 gauge rifle. I liked target practice—never was interested in killing anything except mice and rats. One day he did something that made me angry—I don't remember what. I went to get my rifle cartridges out of the kitchen cabinet, where I kept them, but they weren't there. I made up my mind that when I was fifteen years old, I'd kill him. He died when I was thirteen."

ALTHOUGH FINLEY LEVEL, Pearl's second husband, only had a fourth grade education, he could add a string of numbers in his head and had a mind for business. Daniel affectionately called him Fessor. From the money he saved working night and day as a molder in the foundry he bought some houses and land. Among his investments was a pool room with upstairs living quarters, where the family lived. Because he was a good provider, Pearl was able to quit her cleaning job at the hospital.

During the 1920s pool rooms weren't considered respectable, but Fessor ran a clean place. Daniel spent many hours there, learning to play pool, racking the balls, working behind the counter. Frequently the arrival of an expert created additional excitement, and he joined the customers as they stood around watching. When he was almost fourteen Fessor and Pearl went to visit Fessor's family in Kentucky and left the boy in charge of the business. Another man worked the place, but Daniel went downstairs every night to take in the receipts and every morning to set everything up.

Until that time he hadn't given much thought to racial segregation and discrimination. Given he had so many friends and managed to find plenty of ways to entertain himself, he didn't see much reason to go outside his neighborhood. But at around age thirteen, he began to recognize his special abilities, especially in sports, and took notice that white classmates who weren't as athletic played on school sports teams, while he wasn't allowed to.

The junior high basketball coach, Lyman Libolt, took a special interest in him, and as a result of the coach's efforts Daniel became the first Negro to play on the school's basketball team. But among white Hoosiers basketball had sacred status and a whites-only tradition. In his eighties, Daniel still felt the pain of his first inter-scholastic basketball game.

Fessor had dropped him off in front of the Y.M.C.A. An early snow crunched under his feet, and he could see his breath as he made his way up the sidewalk. Once inside the warmth of the building, everyone else seemed to know which direction to head, so Daniel moved along with teammates, making his contribution to the whoops and hollers that bounced off corridor walls. The group started to enter the locker room.

"Hey, you—kid—you can't go in there." A white man standing by the door pointed at Daniel.

"Why not?"

"Just can't," the man said. As if the matter were settled, he returned to the conversation he'd been having with a woman.

Daniel felt his chest tighten. He tugged on the man's sleeve. His adolescent voice quivered. "But I'm on this team. We're playing tonight."

"Well, you'll have to change into your uniform someplace else. Coloreds aren't allowed in there."

The other boys looked on curiously for a moment, then making undistinguishable mutterings, they entered the locker room without him. Bewildered, Daniel stood near the doorway, looking back and forth, first at the man then at the locker room door.

He searched for Coach Libolt, who would certainly tell this man to let in one of the team's best players. But there was no sign of the coach. Daniel needed to be outside, out where he could think clearly. Walking with a deliberateness belying his insecurities, he pushed his way against the current, through the crowd of spectators entering the building.

As he stepped off the sidewalk, the dampness of the snow penetrated his shoes, the coldness of the evening pierced his spirit. He retreated into the shadows of the building and crept along its parameter until a dark alcove provided a private space. Shivering, he pulled off his shirt and trousers and put on the uniform. Briefly tears blurred his vision, but they gave way to a determination to master his emotions.

Minutes later, carrying street clothes into the gym, he vowed that he would show them all. He'd be the best player on the court.

TEXTBOOKS AT SCHOOL praised the lives of men such as Washington and Jefferson, told how Lincoln had freed the slaves. Crispus Attucks and Benjamin Banneker were mentioned, but none of Daniel's teachers ever identified them as Negroes. Since no pictures accompanied the text, he assumed they were white too.

He learned differently at the Thompson Center. A community venue for the city's black youth, the center offered dances, a Negro History Club, and movies produced by black film makers with black actors. Outside speakers told of an ancestry that extended back to Africa and of the works of Negro writers and artists.

Located in an old fire station, the Thompson Center had a reading room, a large area in the back with a cement floor where children could play, and a large upstairs room used as a gym. Outdoors there were tennis courts, the only ones in town that Negroes had access to. An energetic drama program offered the opportunity for people of all ages to perform.

The man most instrumental in organizing the Thompson Center was Walter Dennis, one of Richmond's two Negro mail carriers, a prestigious job when nearly all the black men in town worked in factories or in the homes of white families. Dennis put much of his own money into getting it started, even paid the salary of a social worker.

With abilities and ambitions but no outlet in the wider community, African Americans in Richmond became resourceful in developing their own social world. The Center played an important role in Daniel's maturation, first as a setting for sports, education, and social interaction; later, during college, a place to earn money for tuition.

CLARA BOW, THE It Girl, the flappers. Adolescence having awakened his awareness of girls, Daniel began to notice changes the roaring twenties brought to female attire. One day they were wearing long dresses; the next thing he knew part of their legs was visible. He was disappointed when fashion began to dictate that breasts, which he'd started to admire, be flattened. And girls were cutting their hair short, a brazen change.

He discovered he had a way with girls. His friend Terrell used to say that wherever Daniel went, you could find a bunch of girls, and he, Terrell, liked hanging around because he always got whoever was left.

Daniel was in seventh grade, Mildred in eighth, the year he started carrying her books home from school. She combined all the attributes he liked in a girl: intelligence, independence, and, of course, good looks. When she went to high school for ninth grade, Daniel languished every day over the separation. He could hardly wait for the following fall when he'd move up to ninth grade and be able to see her during the day. But that year school policy changed, and ninth graders had to stay in the junior high building.

Finally, after two years of being apart, Daniel could parade down the halls of the high school with his girl. And parade he did, for Mildred, having already been there two years, had practically every black boy admiring her.

The romance lasted through high school. Mildred graduated in 1925 and moved to Chicago, where she worked for the *Chicago Defender*, a nationally known black newspaper. For the next few years, whenever she returned to Richmond to visit her mother, she and Daniel spent as much time together as they could.

It was a friendship that would continue over their lifetimes. Shortly after Daniel and Anna moved to Mexico, he invited Mildred and her husband to visit. In 1973 they came.

MUMBLE PEG, AD hoc boxing rings, baseball games in the sandlot—Daniel was accustomed to being the organizer, everybody's pal, whether they were Italian, German, Jewish, or Negro. So he was unprepared for the friendship challenges of high school. Because clubs excluded black students, Mr. Naff, a teacher, organized one for Negro boys. Not liking the segregated structure it reinforced, Daniel decided not to join. The Negro boys accused him of being *too white* to be in their club.

His relationships with white boys were even worse. Organized sports were their turf, and they didn't like his intruding. He managed to run track and play baseball all three years of high school, but no Negroes played basketball, a contact sport. Attending each home game, he watched with bitterness as white boys he'd played with in junior high became school heroes. When, in his senior year, he found the courage to defy the tradition and try out for basketball, the Richmond newspaper ran an article about the "colored boy who made good."

Years later, in his home in Mexico City, he still had his high school yearbooks. In every one—for the classes of 1925, '26, and '27—photos of black students were placed at the end of each class section. His senior year the caption beside his picture read: "If Daniel would only use his head as much as he does those dark eyes." That year he appeared in photos of track and baseball teams but not with the basketball team. Decades later he still resented the coach's excuse: "I forgot to call you down when the picture was taken."

Scrutinizing his classmates, black and white, he saw he was more capable academically than most of them. He was especially strong in the sciences and after taking all the chemistry courses the school offered, he studied advanced chemistry as a tutorial. Yet no teacher ever mentioned college to him, and his shrunken circle of friends considered his talk of higher education bragging.

At school, opportunities to be president or captain didn't exist, but within the black church he discovered his gifts for leadership. Sundays were filled with activity: church services in the morning, Sunday school in the afternoon, and in the evening Christian Endeavor for the young people. As he got older, the oratory contests and special programs of Christian Endeavor gave him a setting to develop skills he wouldn't have been able to cultivate otherwise.

Every Sunday evening, after Christian Endeavor, all the young people went to Mrs. Cramer's home. The seventy-year-old hostess would roll back the rugs, wind up the victrola, and encourage everybody to dance. There were, of course, chaperons.

Daniel: "I joined the church when I was nineteen. When Rev. Black talked to me about joining, I told him I liked to dance and play cards, and I wasn't ready to give them up. He said, 'Son, don't think of the things you can't do as a Christian; think of the things you can do.' But as I got older I began to ask questions you weren't supposed to ask. At this stage in my life I feel it's the way you live that's important. If you can live decently without attending church and listening to sermons, that's fine. Living a decent life is something you can do by yourself. People don't need a church or minister to prod them along. Either you live by religious principles, or you don't."

The Thompson Center would *not* have shown *Birth of a Nation* (1915). The film was released when Daniel was six years old. Using the camera in ways that were groundbreaking at the time, it became one of the most widely viewed movies of all time. While acknowledging that the individuals were fictional, filmmaker Griffith would have viewers believe that the story was built upon historical fact.

The South is in disarray after the Civil War, during Reconstruction. Newly freed slaves (all played by white actors in blackface) vote twice at the polls while respectable white citizens are prevented from voting at all. Chaos results. Chaos in the legislature, where newly elected black men prop their bare feet on the desks, drink whiskey from flasks, and eat chicken legs. Chaos in the streets, where swaggering blacks tote guns and push whites off the sidewalk. Worst of all, chaos in the social order, for one of the first bills passed by the new legislature (which has a black majority) is that marriage between the races will now be legal. One clear message of the movie is that oversexed black men have been waiting a long time to get their hands on pure white women.

Finally, as if they're the U.S. cavalry about to save the fort, a throng of KKK horsemen arrives, saving the white woman held captive by a diabolical mulatto, then disarming the blacks. Life in this southern town can return to peace, a peace overseen by a giant figure of Jesus looming in the heavens.

Some historians consider the film a contributing factor to the Klan's rebirth in the 1920s. This time its membership totaled around four million. The Indiana KKK became the most powerful state branch in the country, with a membership of nearly half a million.

In *Women of the Klan,* Kathleen M. Blee writes of the KKK's success at co-opting religion in Indiana. It was a period of immigration and migration, many of the new arrivals from predominantly Catholic nations across the ocean. The Klan decried their foreignness, claiming they were loyal to the Pope, brought un-American values, and were taking the jobs of real Americans. At the same time blacks migrating from the South to the industrial North were accused of supplanting hard-working whites in the job market.

White ministers, convinced that both Protestantism and American values were under siege, preached on the Klan's behalf. The Women's Christian Temperance Union absorbed the Klan's xenophobia and connected the evils of alcohol with Catholics and immigrants. Quakers, too, as social activists pressing for temperance, extolled KKK support of Prohibition and its campaign against drunkenness.

When they were trying to establish new chapters in towns, Klan organizers, called kleagles, were instructed to go first to a Quaker meeting. Perhaps their most stellar Quaker recruit was Daisy Douglas Barr, a woman from Muncie, Indiana, widely known in the 1920s for her ability as an orator. Likely attracted to the Klan's positions on alcohol and immigration, and not offended by its anti-black convictions, she rose to become head of the national Women's Ku Klux Klan. Throughout Indiana she drew large crowds whenever she spoke. She once told a gathering in Marion, Indiana, "If Christ were on earth at the present time he would certainly join the Klan."[1] Richmond was a Klan stronghold.

Chapter 3

W HAT ABOUT HER *life could possibly interest a reader?*
*Daniel—his was the exciting life, his struggles against racism
the inspiration readers will look for. Besides, he's the one with
the story teller's instincts. A memory for details too, the kind that help you
picture a place and the people, like he's produced a movie and wants you to
see every scene. A good example of how the rift developed between them: his
ability to engage in conversation and tell a story, her holding back, waiting
for a signal that includes her.*

*Where should she start? It would seem logical that the narrative begin
with her birth. Or maybe with memories, faint as they are. Should she start
with her mother's hardships, which she only knows through Violet?*

*The rescue. A story she heard so often that it seems a memory. The first
rescue, she might say, for Violet rescued her several times. Daniel—he
emancipated her, boldly climbing up tangled tower vines then carrying her in
his strong arms back down and into a new life, which was rather like being
rescued. At least that's what she thought at the time. Yet rescue isn't the
theme of her life, for by the time she went to live with Violet and George,
even at the age of thirteen, she already understood what it meant to take care
of herself, make her own decisions. She recognized even at that young age that
rescue is a myth.*

*Yet she can think of no better way to begin than with a winter day she
does not remember, when the sun was dazzling, and the air hinted of
approaching spring.*

WHILE HER MOTHER hung laundry on the line, Anna, wearing a
bright red coat, explored the back yard. One thing after another
captured the toddler's attention: a cluster of brown leaves, which
made a rustling sound when she scattered them with her feet; a
rock that was big enough to climb up on, then jump from, climb
back on, jump again; a narrow tire leaning against the shed, with
ridges to be traced by tiny fingers; a gate with a latch that went
up and down, up and down, clanging each time it hit the metal

post. In the distance a long, black rope swayed back and forth. Anna pushed against the gate. It opened and she walked through, heading toward the hypnotizing pendulum.

Suddenly she felt herself being snatched up and carried along so that her head and arms dangled in the air. Squeezed so tightly she could scarcely catch her breath, she still managed to shriek her indignation. When the thwarter of her exploration finally stopped, Anna looked up and saw that it was Violet who had such a firm hold of her.

Years later, whenever the sisters reminisced, Violet never failed to ask, "Remember when you wandered out into the pasture and a bull was charging you, and I got there just in time to whisk you away?" Of course she didn't.

What would childhood have been like without Violet? Fifteen years her senior, Violet combined a big sister's delight with the maternal instincts of a young woman. And given the later interruptions to a happy childhood, what pleasant memories would Anna have without the cadre of older cousins who entertained her? When she regularly accompanied them down the long, tree-lined lane, her blond curls bounced, her bright eyes sparkled, her laugh was the heartfelt laugh of a little girl in love with life. Sometimes they carried her piggyback; sometimes they pulled her in a homemade wagon. Later she wondered whether the lane was actually as long or her cousins as big as they had seemed through little-girl eyes. Even if her perceptions of size were faulty, the walks provided a glorious time in which she experienced the love of those she looked up to. Cousins, brother, and sisters heaped attention and affection upon her, the family's blond-haired, hazel-eyed, youngest member.

BOTH SIDES OF Anna's family were of German descent and had for generations been members of the Church of the Brethren. Brethren tended to settle in geographic clusters, in a manner similar to the Amish and Mennonites, who emerged from the same historical religious movement. Anna spent her younger years in and around the western Ohio town of Lima, in a strict environment that did not allow dancing, card playing, drinking, or smoking.

Most of her knowledge about her childhood and ancestry came from Violet. In February of 1901 their mother, Nellie Brubaker, from northern Ohio, married their father, Walter Harley, the oldest son of Mary Ann and Jacob Harley, of Lima, Ohio. Nellie and Walter had met at Manchester College (in Indiana), where he took a business course and she prepared for teaching. After the wedding the couple headed south, a day's journey by buggy, to their new farm. A wedding gift from Walter's parents, it adjoined the one he had grown up on.

Until her arrival the day after the wedding, Nellie hadn't seen her new home. Every time she asked Walter to tell her about the house, he'd describe the rich soil and generous spring. In spite of her suspicions that he was deliberately withholding the truth to spare her, she was unprepared for the disappointment. The house's four small rooms were cramped and dismal.

Not to be defeated by ugliness, she set about making her home as cheerful as possible. With the help of the hired hand she papered the dreary walls with dainty floral patterns and laid linoleum on the rough wide floor planks. She brightened the rooms with colorful curtains. It was in this house that Nellie gave birth to five children: two daughters, Violet and Ruth, born in 1902 and 1906, a son, Ralph, born in 1904, and a little girl who died at birth. Anna was born in June, 1917.

Four years after their marriage, without consulting Nellie, Walter put up a large, modern barn. Fifteen more years passed before he got around to constructing a modern house with a coal furnace, indoor plumbing, and electricity.

A letter written in faded pencil with a flowing, feminine style was among Anna's keepsakes. Corresponding with a sister in northern Ohio, Nellie mentioned neither happiness nor sadness, only telling of crops to be planted, the illnesses of the children, and recent weather. "I think of you often, my sister and friend," Nellie wrote in the last sentence, "and wish we could be together." Perhaps her sister was able to read between the lines: that life with Walter was difficult.

Between her tenderness and the *Inglenook Cookbook's* home remedies, Nellie managed to keep her children healthy and happy. A slice of heavily peppered smoked bacon stitched to a piece of flannel and placed at the neck healed sore throats. A ready lap and a gentle hand healed hurt feelings.

DURING THE JULY Anna was born, three hundred and fifty miles southwest of Lima, in East St. Louis, white workers vented their frustrations on the city's African-American population. Management in the meat processing and manufacturing plants had fired white members and leaders of the emerging unions, replacing them with African-American men who had recently moved to the city from the rural South. Rather than fault management for the loss of their livelihood, labor leaders blamed black men. In July, 1917, convinced that black migrants were threatening their jobs and the safety of the community, whites went berserk, stopping street cars to pull blacks off, firing weapons at them, setting the flimsy shanties they called *home* ablaze.

In the one day of rioting at least thirty-nine African Americans and nine whites were killed,[2] thousands injured, and score of homes in the black section of town destroyed. After the riot fifteen black men who had defended their homes were sentenced to fifteen years in prison; one, a prominent dentist, received a life sentence. Ten white men were sentenced to five years in prison; some of their cohorts spent only a few days in jail.[3] The message had been conveyed: blacks had better head back South.

To Ohio farmers standing outside the grain elevator, the riots probably typified life in the big city. All the violence had to be the fault of *them colored folks*. As Walter joined in these discussions, he likely assumed that the experiences of African Americans and the clashes between labor unions and management had nothing to do with him or his family. Of course he had no way of knowing that his new-born daughter would someday marry a man at the center of such conflicts.

A YEAR APART in school, Violet and Ralph walked to a one-room school house two miles down the road. This time together each day contributed to such a strong emotional attachment that when Violet graduated from eighth grade, she couldn't bear the thought of entering high school without her brother. Besides, she had no transportation to the school, located nine miles away in town. She decided to spend an extra year in eighth grade. The following fall, soon after Anna was born, the family bought a new Model T Ford, which Violet drove to school, even in the worst weather. In those days, when automobiles were still a recent invention, drivers' licenses weren't required.

Barely over the age of two, Anna couldn't tell time, but she recognized by the position of the hands on the clock when to ask her mother to help her put on her coat and mittens. Insulated from the cold, she headed out the door and down the long lane. To a passer-by the little girl standing by the road must have looked forlorn, but Anna's thoughts were ones of happy anticipation, especially when the Model T came into sight. When it pulled off the gravel road and stopped, Ralph reached down to lift her onto his lap. On the trip up the lane, Anna basked in the attention of her big brother and sister.

HER MOTHER WAS crying; Violet was crying; people were going in and out of the house. Aunt May came from the adjoining farm, "to see what I can do to help," she said. Her way of helping was to gather some of Anna's clothes and take the child home with her.

Always before, staying overnight at her cousins' house had been a special occasion, marked by gaiety and play. Now, instead of bouncing her around in their usual boisterous manner, everyone played with her quietly. She was frightened with no discernable source of her fright, wary without a defined threat. When she stood by the door, crying to go home, Aunt May pulled her away and said her mother had too much on her mind.

Finally taken back home, she found the front parlor filled with people speaking to each other in soft tones, stepping every now and then into the adjoining room, returning with tears in their eyes. Anna pushed her way between them, her distressed eyes searching for her mother. There she was, in the high-backed rocking chair. Anna took no notice of Nellie's gaunt face or puffy eyes; the child saw only the empty lap, a familiar soft hollow in which she could securely nestle. Her mother clung to her tightly, spoke gently to her, and rocked her back and forth, back and forth. The ominous mood that pervaded everything familiar to Anna was for the moment subdued.

As soon as those who were not relatives left the house, aunts, uncles, and cousins took filled plates into the parlor or kitchen. Nearly every woman in the church had brought something over to eat. On any other occasion such a collection of food would have been a feast of fellowship; a cousin would have teasingly tugged on Anna's curls; others would have tested their mothers' patience by seeing how boisterously they could play inside the house; everyone would have eaten heartily of the sumptuous bounty of summer's gardens. On this day, though, the voices were subdued, appetites meager. Panic seized Anna when Aunt May softly said, "It's time for us to go back home, Anna." How could Mama let Aunt May take her away?

Again time had no meaning; days spent with her aunt, uncle, and cousins seemed endless. Finally she was allowed to return home, but things were different. When she asked where Ralph was, Violet cried. For a while no one said much to her; no one tried to make her laugh.

Later she came to understand that her brother, Ralph, had drowned while swimming with some friends at a gravel quarry. And eventually she recognized what a profound loss his death was for both her mother and Violet. During the year that followed, Nellie maintained a strength that was almost beyond her. Surely Anna had been sent to her as a comfort, she said, recalling when at forty-one she'd been distraught over learning she was pregnant. Violet recalled her mother also comforting herself by saying, "All things work together for good to those who love the Lord," and "Perhaps he would not have turned out to be a good man."

The innumerable tasks of a farm wife still had to be done, and there was still a young child to care for. Nellie was grateful that Violet decided to stay home that year instead of going on to college as she'd planned. And Ruth was a quiet, hard-working sixteen-year-old who did what she could to help.

~~~

IN THE YEARS they'd been married, Walter had not asked Nellie's opinion, nor had he informed her, about business transactions. Soon after Anna's birth, Nellie was tilling the garden for planting when several horse-drawn wagons loaded with young calves paraded up the lane. This was the first she knew Walter had borrowed money to purchase purebred cattle. About three years later, less than a year after Ralph's death, the investment failed. Not only did Walter lose the herd, but the farm too.

He wasn't alone in his miscalculations. During World War I a high demand for agricultural products had motivated many farmers to buy more land, more equipment, in Walter's case more cattle. As a result farmers accrued debts they could not later repay and produced an overabundance of food. When prices for agricultural products fell, many lost their land.

No one in the family ever learned how Walter felt about the loss, but for Nellie, the total collapse of the family's finances meant a disgrace and an uncertainty she could hardly bear. As the oldest daughter, Violet was particularly sensitive to the hurt her mother suffered. She told Anna that she didn't remember whether it was after Ralph's death or after it was clear they would lose the farm, but she vividly recalled waking up one night and hearing her mother out in the yard, crying hysterically.

Nellie's life as an adult was not easy. She left close family ties to marry a man who considered her neither a partner nor a companion. He was stubborn and hot-tempered. She lost a baby, her teenage son, her home, and all financial security. Although it was humiliating, she asked her parents for a loan to buy a house in the nearby town of New Freedom. They insisted the house be put in her name, a wise decision it turned out to be. Walter got a job sanding floors and, except for one more foray into owning his own business, continued to earn his living that way until he became old.

CURIOUS AT FIRST about what the women were doing, six-year-old Anna watched her aunt put copper pennies in the bottom of the cast-iron pot that hung outside over an open fire. A short time later, after her mother and another woman skimmed the cider and added apples and sugar, the small group of women took turns stirring the beginnings of apple butter. Soon the children lost interest and headed for the woods. The dog's excited barks and the cousins' shrieks as they romped in the fallen leaves generated an autumn intoxication. Not until they grew hungry did the children return to the house.

As they stepped out of the woods, they saw the kettle still hanging over the fire but no one stirring it. The women, they discovered, were inside, standing around the bed on which Nellie lay, unable to move or talk. It was in 1923, less than two years after the family had moved into town, that Nellie suffered a stroke at her sister-in-law's house. For the next nine months Anna was allowed into her mother's bedroom only twice a day, and then under the stern-faced supervision of her grandmother. Blurred images of an ambulance driving her mother home, of sitting alone in the rocking chair by the wood stove in the kitchen, Violet's occasional visit from college, and continuous admonitions by her grandmother to play quietly—these became Anna's memories of the last year of her mother's life.

Nellie died at the age of forty-eight. Anna had turned seven that summer.

When Violet married in 1926, she and her husband, George, moved in with Walter and the two younger girls, Ruth and Anna, intending to help out. Violet, though, found her father hard to get along with. The arrangement only lasted a few months.

Anna: "I have few memories of my mother prior to the stroke. As with Papa, my knowledge of her has come primarily from Violet, who remembers her as a wonderful person. She's always blamed our father for Mama's unhappiness. For years people spoke of what a good woman she was. Even when I went to college, the president remembered her as the fine woman who had been his Sunday school teacher when he was a boy in northern Ohio."

FOR NO PARTICULAR reason Anna counted the steps leading to the front porch of Mrs. Eberly's house. One, two, three, four. Actually, Mrs. Eberly wasn't her name anymore. It was Mrs. Harley now that she and Papa had married. And this wasn't just *her* house. For Mrs. Eberly—no, Mrs. Harley—her children, and

Papa, this was home. It was supposed to be Anna's home now, too, but she didn't believe that could ever be.

Home meant *her* family: Violet, Ruth, and Papa—oh, and George, of course. Except for her and Papa, though, everyone lived over in Richmond, Indiana. Violet and George had set up a tent in Glen Miller Park, while George worked on the hospital construction project. Ruth, who had a job as a store clerk, lived in the tent too. When George finished that job, they would all be together again—Violet, George, Ruth, Papa, and her, Anna dreamed.

Up the four steps she carried her most precious possessions: her rag doll, Tessie, which she'd had as long as she could remember, her favorite book, *A Girl of the Limberlost,* and the small collection of ceramic animals Violet had started for her. It was a strange feeling, moving into someone else's house. She'd be sharing a bedroom with a girl, ten years old like her, who wasn't a sister, yet *was* a sister. Every day she'd have to talk with this woman who wasn't her mother, yet *was* her mother. She didn't want a new sister or a new mother, or a new brother, either. Not that these people were strangers—they were all members of the same church; and Sarah and Joseph both went to the school she attended. So she'd known them all her life, she guessed. But they certainly weren't family.

In the parlor Sarah and Joseph stood beside their mother, seated in the armchair. Walter walked over, shyly put his hand on his new wife's shoulder, and spoke with her and her children. Most any other observer would have noticed his awkwardness, but watching from the doorway, Anna's eyes only saw that he was getting along splendidly with his new family. She waited for some signal that would draw her into the cluster. If this girl and boy belonged to Mrs. Eberly—no, Mrs. Harley—if Papa was now the father of this family, then everyone belonged to someone. Everyone but her.

As energetic and hard working as Bessie Harley was, one would have expected her to be slender. Not that she was fat, just plump, with a large bosom and slightly flabby arms. In spite of a friendly disposition and a soft body that suggested an affectionate nature, Bessie stayed so busy she didn't have time to be particularly tender. In her first marriage she'd supplemented her minister husband's income by taking in laundry, an enterprise that supported her and the children after his death. When she married Walter she continued to do the washing and ironing for several Lima families. In addition to this strenuous physical work and her own household duties, she taught a Sunday school class and headed the Ladies' Aid Society at church.

So the family operated in much the way a small, efficiently run business might function, with Bessie as the manager. Had Walter been wiser, he would have relied on his new wife's managerial instincts when he invested in a welding business. But making unilateral decisions was his style, and subsequently his second business venture also failed.

IT WASN'T THAT she felt like Cinderella, Anna thought as she scrubbed the kitchen floor. Doing her and her father's ironing, keeping the kitchen floor clean, and gathering the eggs were hard work but not impossible. Besides, Joseph and Sarah had as many chores as she did. And it wasn't that she had a wicked step-mother. No, she couldn't complain about being mistreated. She had enough to eat and decent clothes to wear. No one in the family was hard to get along with.

Leaning back on her haunches to rest, she swept a blond lock from her face with a wet hand. She had everything she needed; that was obvious. What she didn't have, though, was the feeling of belonging to someone. Every day, when Papa came home from sanding floors, he cleaned up then sat down to supper. Other than "pass the potatoes," there was little conversation from his end of the table. After supper he usually went into the living room and spent the evening sleeping in the green overstuffed chair. He never hugged Anna or held her on his lap as he sat in the big chair. He never asked questions about how she was doing in school or what she was thinking. And the only question her step-mother had time to direct was, "Did you do your chores?"

Anna couldn't get over the feeling of being the step-child, always treated with consideration but never with affection. Violet and George had recently taken off for Florida, where they would wait tables for the winter, and Ruth was in college. A tear escaped as Anna recalled her dream of their being a family.

Anna: "For a while I was resigned to the family situation. I'm unsure of why I became unhappy. It seems now that the atmosphere was competitive—perhaps I was competing with her children for her attention. I never could get over the feeling of being an outsider."

FOLLOWING BRIEF PERIODS of living in a tent in Richmond and waiting tables in Florida, George and Violet settled into young adulthood with a home and, for George, a job. He was manager of a Kroger grocery store in Brookville, Ohio, where weekdays he rented a room. Violet stayed in their Richmond home, forty miles away, just over the state line.

Lonely much of the time, she invited Anna to spend the summer of 1930. Escape—that's what Anna thought of the idea. Not from a prisonlike atmosphere but from insignificance. Three days before she was scheduled to leave, she'd already packed her suitcase.

Most afternoons, after completing household chores, the sisters, ages twenty-eight and thirteen, read in the shade of a large oak tree in the back yard. Sometimes they went to movies. One week, when Violet taught a class at Daily Vacation Bible School, Anna assisted.

Several years later Violet would be among the first to own a Bendix automatic washing machine. In 1930, however, she had a wringer washer and followed the home-laundry regimen of many housewives: wash on Monday, iron on Tuesday.

IT WAS A MONDAY. To keep George's pants from floating to the water's surface, Anna tamped them down with a short wooden paddle. Next to her Violet transferred items one at a time from the second rinse tub through electric powered rollers, into a bushel basket lined in oilcloth. She never allowed Anna to do this. Too often rollers crushed women's fingers, hands, entire arms even. Next, Violet on one side, Anna on the other, the two carried the basket laden with wet clothes from the basement, up a short flight of steps leading directly to the backyard.

Anna shook wrinkles out of George's shirts and underwear, and hung them on the line. Dare she ask? It would put her sister in an awkward position, having to say yes or no. But if she didn't ask… By the time the basket was empty, she'd made up her mind.

She stepped closer to Violet. "I'd like to tell you something," she said barely above a whisper. "I'd prefer living with you."

At first Violet's reply was neither yes nor no, but "Mmm." Anna studied her face for a clue. What did sucked-in jaws and a crooked mouth mean?

"Let me talk with George about this, over the weekend," Violet finally said.

But before George returned to Richmond a letter arrived.

Dear Violet,

It has been a hot summer, hasn't it? Not too good for the farmers with the draught and all. Lucky we don't have to depend on the weather for our livelihood.

The reason I am writing is this. I think it would be a good idea if Anna stayed with you a while longer as Walter is going to Oklahoma for a spell. I am sure she would be better off there.

I hope you and your family are doing well. The children and I send our regards to Anna.

Yours truly,
Bessie[4]

Several months passed before Anna and Violet learned that Walter had gone to Oklahoma not just for a trip but to live. Bessie had kicked him out of the house. Given the Church of the Brethren's strong disapproval of divorce, the reasons for seeking one had to be extreme and substantiated. Apparently Bessie's met those criteria. Doubting Walter's faithfulness, she'd hired a detective, who confirmed her suspicions. The marriage had lasted three years. Bessie was allowed to remain in fellowship with the Brethren, but of course, in a small conservative community such as Lima, the Harley name must have been mentioned over many a backyard fence.

In a letter to the author, one of Bessie's nephews recalled that his father, who performed the marriage ceremony, feared she was getting married more for security than for love. "I remember few details of their life together. I recall that Aunt Bessie accused him of infidelity and abuse. The two of them were really quite incompatible from the start. Our family felt that Anna suffered, which contributed to an already evident insecurity. Aunt Bessie later moved to Michigan, where she died in 1935."

Except for a brief period when Walter temporarily stayed with Daniel and her, Anna never lived with her father again.

BY THE TIME school started in the fall of 1930, Violet and Anna had moved from Richmond to join George in Brookville, Ohio, a small town of about twelve hundred people. Anna entered eighth grade that fall and attended all of high school in the same building.

A fair-skinned man with a full face and slightly bulging eyes, George had an earnest demeanor but could quickly break into a smile. He was a steady sort, dependable but quiet and unassertive. Perhaps because he was motivated by a background of economic hardship, he worked long hours and carried a heavy responsibility. (In the 1940s he would open his own corner grocery store in Richmond.)

Except for her slender build, Violet didn't much resemble Anna. She had dark eyes and dark hair, and whereas Anna, when she became an adult, walked with fluidity and an erect posture, Violet seemed to dart. Her mind moved just as quickly. Not only was she intent upon communication, sharing thoughts many would have kept to themselves, she was resolute in her determination to understand people. During her two years of college she'd become fascinated with psychology, still a young science, which she applied to interpret most any interaction or behavior. Dizzy from weaving in and out of everyone's psyche, she often gave the impression of being disoriented or scatterbrained. Yet it was her constant analyzing that made her aware of Anna's gifts and needs.

Although she had a proclivity towards constant motion, Violet understood the importance of, and was capable of, sitting down and listening. Because she was an excellent surrogate mother, who understood both Anna's childlike need for nurture and her adolescent craving for independence, Anna felt grateful to Violet throughout her life.

SIXTY-FIVE MILES northwest of Richmond is the town of Marion. In August, 1930, during Anna's summer with Violet, two African-American men, Thomas Shipp and Abram Smith, were arrested for the robbery and murder of a white man and the rape of his white girlfriend. (Later, the woman said she had not been raped.) A mob broke into the jail and lynched the two men. A photographer took a picture, a gruesome shot of a white crowd gathered around two dead black men hanging from a tree. Images of that event inspired the song "Strange Fruit," made famous by Billie Holiday.

"RADIO CAME," VIOLET wrote in her June 18, 1931, diary entry. Not the kind that rested on a table or small stand, but a console model, a piece of furniture so large that it had to be reckoned with in arranging the living room. "Don't like cabinet so very well."

Radio was new enough that the 1930 census had a column designating whether households owned one. Evenings Violet and Anna mended or embroidered as they sat listening to the music of Rudy Vallee and his Connecticut Yankees. They laughed out loud at the antics of *Amos 'n' Andy,* two white men playing the roles of uneducated black men.

And they listened to Lowell Thomas report on the trials of the Scottsboro Boys. To African-Americans in the South, it was a familiar sequence of events: accusations of black men taking liberties with white women, jail in a small town (in this case, Scottsboro, Alabama), lynch mobs, trial by an all-white jury. Nine young black men ranging in age from thirteen to nineteen, had, like many others during the Depression, been riding the rails. In March, 1931, near Chattanooga, they got in a fight with a group of white hoboes. When a posse dragged the nine black *boys* off the train, two young women, also riding the rails, accused them of rape. For a while it appeared that all nine of the arrested men would be executed, but the NAACP and the Communist Party took on the cause, spreading word of the injustice all around the country. Especially in the North many people, black and white, were convinced the charge of rape was a frame-up.

Anna didn't know any Negroes, but was sure that if she did, she wouldn't hate them the way those people in Alabama did. Jesus had said we are to love our neighbor as ourselves, and when asked, "Who is my neighbor?" he'd told the story of the Good Samaritan. The answer to the question, she decided, was that the young men imprisoned in Alabama were her neighbors.

THOUGH VIOLET MADE no mention of the financial climate in her diary of 1931, one of the worst years of the Great Depression, she did occasionally record sales at the grocery George managed. "Store $573," "reached $800 mark." (In 1930 a dozen eggs cost eighteen cents, a loaf of bread a nickel.) But the couple seems to have been doing well enough that in April she wrote, "Launching a loafing time. Hired washing." In September, 1931, on a trip to Dayton, George bought a new suit, and in keeping with the recent trend of affordable ready-to-wear clothes, as opposed to handmade ones, Anna "got hat, dresses, etc."

The diary makes no mention of Violet's strong desire to start a family or of past miscarriages. Perhaps because she feared this one would end like the others, she didn't even record that she was pregnant. All of a sudden on a January Saturday in 1932, she wrote, "Joyce arrived. George and Anna think she is wonderful."

FACES SCRUBBED, WEARING clean starched and ironed dresses—simple yet feminine, with snug waists and hemlines mid-shin—Anna and her friends gathered in the church foyer before Opening Exercises. Entering the sanctuary together, models of female adolescent piety, they filed into a pew.

Hands folded in their laps, they listened to the opening prayer, scripture, a few thoughts, a closing prayer, everything brought to a conclusion by the Sunday School Superintendent saying in his most officious voice, "We will now depart for our Sunday school hour." The girls filed back out the pew and walked in pairs down the hallway to their class. A few boldly looked into the room where the boys met.

Sister Barnhart was a warm, caring teacher whose demeanor made it clear that the girls need not be self-conscious in their discussions or afraid to ask honest questions. Earnestly they discussed loving your neighbor, forgiving someone seventy times seven, and judging "not that ye be not judged." More than fifty years later Anna still had the linen Bible bookmark on which, as a girl, she had embroidered "Love Never Faileth."

In contrast to her feelings of loss and marginality in previous years, the camaraderie of Sunday school classes and church camp in the summers began to draw Anna out of herself.

Anna: "My experiences of being loved and accepted within the church and community made me assume that everyone did, indeed, belong to the family of God. I believed all those principles the church taught: Love your neighbor. We are all brothers and sisters. Largely because of the church's teachings, my attitude towards people has always been centered around accepting individuals.

"It never occurred to me that it's easier to talk of love and spreading kindness when the group is homogeneous. It never occurred to me that it might be *wrong* to have a close relationship with someone of a different race. It came as a complete surprise when I later discovered that the people who had taught me to accept everyone didn't really believe that themselves. What I don't understand is how I came to believe what they said when they didn't."

"ANNA AND HER friends went to a show," Violet recorded several times in her diary.

Cinema of the thirties created a new female archetype.[5] Played by stars such as Barbara Stanwyck and Katharine Hepburn, the ideal woman of that decade was intelligent, adventuresome, and restless. Rather than submissively waiting for life to improve, she applied her intellect and adventurous spirit. A girl who came from humble beginnings could rise in society; one who held fast to her convictions reaped the rewards. She could get along without a man—for a while, that is—but eventually the right one would come her way.

Maybe Anna and her friends sat in a dark theater deciding they wanted to be like those independent, free-thinking women on the screen.

Chapter 4

*T*HEY'RE FAMILIAR WORDS, *spoken over supper: Daniel's intolerance for weak politicians, young people dressing like slobs, men who can't hold down a job. Especially when there's a guest, she feels the need to moderate his tone. If he knew what others have been through, he'd be more sympathetic, she says. Well, he's been through a lot too, he says.*

Always clear about his intended conclusion, he presents his arguments in a logical, organized way. Point a leads to point b to point c. She'd consider him a rational thinker had she not often heard his less rational opinions.

She, on the other hand—she knows she approaches a discussion with emotion, and though she gets easily sidetracked, skipping from a to d and back to c, she's still a formidable opponent. He used to say that's what he liked about her: that she could think for herself. Yet when she does, he responds in anger.

For five years the son of strong-willed Pearl lived with an emotionally weak step-father who couldn't hold a job and couldn't stand up to his wife. Unable to confront anyone of strength, he exercised control over the only person in his world with less power than he: his step-son, Daniel.

What rage develops in a child who knows he is stronger than the man who beats him. What rage must accumulate in a Negro who knows he's more intelligent and more skilled than the white supervisor or the white man who gets a better job.

To keep the violence in requires immense self-control.

IT WAS STILL rare for a young black man to attend college, especially one with a nearly exclusively white student body. Only twenty-seven years earlier, in 1900, little more than 2000 African Americans had earned degrees in higher education, the vast majority of them from all-black colleges.[6]

The cost of room, board, and tuition at Earlham for the 1927-28 academic year came to five hundred dollars, three hundred of which Daniel was able to save by living at home.

Fessor, whose investments were doing well, helped out, but Daniel still had to work hard. A movie cost a dime and a hamburger at Fanny's was a nickel, so by comparison raising two hundred dollars presented quite a challenge for a young man right out of high school.

Decades later, when Daniel's students, all from wealthy Mexican families, blamed a busy schedule for not finishing a homework assignment, Daniel didn't hesitate to recite his list of responsibilities from college days. In addition to studies, he handled two jobs, one at the Thompson Center (the Negro community center) where he did everything from supervising younger children to selling refreshments behind the counter. Nights he'd head for the lawnmower manufacturing company to clean the office building until one or two in the morning. The following day began at six, when he'd return to sweep the floors at the Thompson Center. Then it was off to classes.

Prior to registering he'd never been on campus. Only five miles from home and with a liberal tradition, it was, nonetheless, a white world. His friend Arthur had once been arrested by an Earlham police officer. There were myriad offenses for which the officer could arrest people—among them arson, dissecting a human body unlawfully, kidnapping, defacing tombstones, and working on Sunday. Apparently a person could also be arrested for being a Negro.

In the late twenties Earlham resembled many other liberal-arts, church-related colleges. Campus entertainment might feature the movie, *George Washington: His Life and Times,* or a meeting of the bird club, where a professor accompanied his talk on water birds of the South with slides. In the winter of 1927-28 young men at Earlham were described as having gone *chess crazy.*

DANIEL WALKED ACROSS the shady campus toward the men's dormitory, location of the lounge for Day Lighters, as commuting students were called. He'd prepared for his first day on campus by ordering new gray flannel pants, tan and white spectator shoes, and a waistcoat from the Sears Roebuck catalog. Initial impressions were important.

But already his confidence was being challenged, for though he was pressed for money, other students seemed not to be. The girls in their knee-length pleated skirts, dresses with dropped waists and belts at the hips; the boys in Oxford bags and bow ties—he was guessing everyone else went to Indianapolis to buy the latest in fashion. Well, he decided, more important than what he wore was the self-assurance with which he wore it. He reached up to give his cloth cap a little more tilt.

In front of him, behind him, white students walked in pairs and trios, some in serious conversation, others erupting in a chorus of laughter over a private joke. Just as he was wondering if he would ever be part of any group, two girls approached from behind and adjusted their pace to his.

"Hi. You new on campus?" That's all it took for him to relax his shoulders and smile. By the time he made it to the steps of the men's dorm, he knew their names—Maggie and Gladys—and that they both came from Dayton, Ohio.

Inside the dormitory Daniel climbed the half flight of stairs to the landing, where he was forced to look into the gigantic face of an earnest young man whose portrait attested to his parents having donated a large sum of money in his memory. Up another half flight, down a wide hallway. He paused in front of an open door to take a deep breath.

Upon entering the parlor he removed his hat. Nodding a silent greeting to no one in particular, he immediately judged the room—with Windsor chairs and green velvet sofas supported by Queen Anne legs—not conducive to stretching out his own long legs and taking naps. Most likely the intent was to encourage academic alertness rather than slumber. Which, come to think of it, suited him fine. He planned to excel in his studies. Not that his mother would abide his doing otherwise.

While a small cluster of students conversed on the attributes and deficits of various faculty members, others gathered around a game of chess. Settling into a Windsor chair, its lack of padding offering no hope for comfort, Daniel began to read the first anatomy assignment. He'd just turned to page three when the noisy entrance of another Day Lighter gave him reason to look up and take notice of a burly dark-haired fellow. Immediately the newcomer's gaze fell on Daniel, who feigned indifference and returned his eyes to the anatomy book.

"If I'd known they let those in here, I wouldn't have come to Earlham," the newcomer said.

Daniel acted as if he hadn't heard. He could handle trouble but he wasn't anxious to run into it his first day on campus.

"You know, Yeager, I really don't like sitting in the same room as his kind."

"Stop it, Powell," someone said.

Daniel brought himself to an erect, alert posture. The belligerent Powell slammed his books on a table, shuffled over, and stood before Daniel, arms folded across his chest. "Did you hear me? I don't like being with your kind."

"You can go elsewhere if you wish," Daniel said coldly.

Powell reached down and grabbed the collar of Daniel's shirt with both hands. Thinking a confrontation would be more equal if they were at the same elevation, Daniel started to stand. Powell pushed him back in his chair. Daniel brought his feet up and shoved Powell away. As Powell struggled to maintain balance, Daniel leaped from the chair and started toward him.

Powell was much heavier than Daniel, who at six feet, four inches tipped the scales at 140 pounds, and that after a big Sunday dinner. Stooped in a clench beside an open window, the adversaries both looked for an opportunity to gain the advantage. For the heavier man it would be a moment when he could physically best Daniel; for Daniel it would be when he could outwit Powell. There was a moment of rapid movement that left Daniel lying on his stomach, Powell's weight inexplicably resting on his hip. With an agility perfected in basketball, Daniel raised his torso and jerked his hip. Powell was thrown off balance, landing flat on his back, an indignity that evoked boisterous laughter from the audience. Daniel brushed off his new clothes, grabbed his books, and quickly exited the room.

From then on he studied in the library.

DURING HIS FIRST two years Daniel was the only Negro on campus. Ever mindful that a lost temper or careless word would reflect on the whole race, he maintained constant vigilance over his emotions. Equally taxing was the inquisitiveness of nineteen and twenty-year-olds experimenting with thinking independently. "If my parents knew you were on campus and I was talking to you," a girl from Big Stone Gap, Virginia, told him, "I'd have to go home right away." Refusing to help each soul searcher look at the race problem would provide evidence that *Negroes are unfriendly,* but engaging in such conversations, which he by nature enjoyed, used precious time and energy that he preferred devoting to study or carrying out a normal social life.

Not that a *normal* social life on campus was in any way possible. The Y.M.C.A. offered a Wednesday evening free swim to Earlham students, whites only. Theater parties went to the Tivoli, where Daniel could only sit in the balcony area designated for Negroes. Later in the school year he would have to rely on conversations or the school paper for a description of the May Day breakfast held at a local hotel, where he wasn't welcome. He could only read about the crowning of the Queen of May, her identity kept secret prior to the event, and that she was attended by young women in pastel-colored costumes of medieval design.

HE WAS, AFTER all, a Hoosier and had played basketball since he was big enough to toss and catch a ball. Athletes sprinting from one end of the court to the other, their shouts of encouragement echoing against the gym's high rooftop; rubber soles squeaking as they stopped abruptly; shouts of anger or enthusiasm from the bleachers—he found pleasure even in being a spectator. But he much preferred playing: the adrenalin rush as he came toe to toe with a competitor, the demands placed on his body for speed, endurance, accuracy.

Daniel went into the first afternoon of scrimmage confident he would make Earlham's team. On the floor he was aggressive, on the bench respectful. Red Stanton, a freckle-faced redhead who was also a freshman, wanted to show his prowess too and was equally aggressive. Red was good, no doubt about it.

An hour or so into practice, Red was guarding Daniel, moving in close, defying Daniel to get around him. Daniel had the ball and was searching for an opening, "Hey, watcha think

you're doing, black boy?" Red taunted. Not only was the word
boy demeaning, but in those days the word *black* was charged.
Daniel, like many Negroes of that time, considered himself
brown, not black. Ignoring Red's derision, he centered his
thoughts on playing exemplary basketball.

The following day, during scrimmage, as Daniel was moving
the ball down court, Red again hovered over him, muttering
under his breath, "Hey, watch it there, black boy." That was it!
Allowing the ball to continue without him, Daniel lunged. As
though attached to a spring, Red staggered backwards before
coming back full force. Mercilessly the two threw punches until
the other players were able to separate them.

Coach Gillian cut Daniel from the squad.

Daniel hadn't let it be known around his circle of
acquaintances that he was going out for basketball, so there was
no need to tell anyone about the humiliation. As he'd done in the
past, he buried the anger and put his energy into his studies.

THE ROARING TWENTIES, the third decade of the twentieth
century, was a period of optimism and prosperity. Women, who
had only recently won the right to vote, cut their hair, raised their
hemlines, entered colleges and universities in record numbers,
and let it be known that like men, they were sexual beings with
sexual desires. Mass produced goods, such as the automobile and
radio, inaugurated an age of consumerism. Highways were built;
homes electrified; indoor plumbing installed. Entertainment and
the arts flourished. Lindbergh's solo non-stop flight across the
Atlantic raised hope that air travel would someday be available
for the wider public.

Even though he had to work harder than most of his
classmates to make tuition payments, Daniel shared the
optimism of the era. At the end of his sophomore year, in the
spring of 1929, he assumed he'd be returning to Earlham in the
fall. But that October the stock market would crash, leaving the
nation's economy in free-fall. In fact, when school let out for the
summer the economy was already shrinking, devaluing Fessor's
investments. Soon Daniel realized he would have to drop out of

college. He was disappointed but confident he would eventually return and earn his diploma.

Indeed, the Great Depression ended up wiping out Fessor's investments that weren't in real estate, and the lawn mower company whose office building Daniel had been cleaning folded. For many African Americans, especially those living in rural areas, poverty was already a way of life. In urban areas an employer forced to lay off workers would lay off Negroes first. The unemployment rate for blacks ranged two to three times that of whites. So it was inevitable that the Negro community of Richmond could no longer afford to support the Thompson Center but had to rely instead on volunteers.

Construction, cement mixing—Daniel spent the next two years working any job he could find, each one short-term and physically grueling. For a while he carried hod. Resting a heavy Y-shaped trough filled with mortar on their shoulders, hod carriers climbed ladders to the various levels of a building, balancing the load with a thick stick pressed against their side. Daniel went home his first day with large open blisters on his shoulders.

Then there were no jobs, and he had nothing to do but hang out. He and his friends would start each day with a swim out at Morton Lake, not an official swimming area. Pools and public beaches were for white residents only. After their swim, even in the hottest summer weather, the group went over to the Thompson Center and played tennis the rest of the day. Evenings the young men competed in a softball league.

In addition to an occasional menial job, Daniel managed to make a little money boxing. Though he weighed only a little over one hundred forty pounds, he once filled in for a heavy-weight fighter who didn't show up. He was knocked out. *Well,* he thought afterward, *I don't have cauliflower ears yet. I don't have any scars, and my mother doesn't want me to box. Now's a good time to let it go.*

DURING DANIEL'S TWO-YEAR absence from Earlham, a student group that had visited Wilberforce, a black college in Ohio, wanted to reciprocate the hospitality. They needed the president's approval. In his office, reading glasses perched on his nose, Dr. Dennis studied their proposal. What topics would the symposium cover, he wanted to know. Marriage between the races would be one, they said.

Following the meeting, the president sent a letter to the group: "While I appreciate that intermarriage might ultimately be the biological answer to race problems, as some scientists think, at present it is absolutely objectionable to the great majority of white people, and however satisfactory between exceptional individuals, it means a life of humiliation and shame for their children. It is a topic which arouses intense prejudice. A public discussion of it by a group of students of mixed races at Earlham is sure to give offense to the community without contributing any proportionate value to the understanding of the serious issues involved."[7]

The black students visited Earlham, but the planning committee substituted a musical program for the symposium.

Mixing the races was an issue Dr. Dennis continued to deal with. In 1943, ten years after Daniel returned and graduated from Earlham, a black male student invited a white female to the winter dance. Calling the young woman into her office, Miss Comstock, Dean of Girls, advised her to renege on the invitation. When word got out, letters representing varying viewpoints began pouring into the president's office. "I have been told," student Earle Estes wrote, "that you and Miss Comstock agreed that no social function at which white and colored students danced together would be sanctioned by the two of you. Truly a remarkable statement, if true, to come from the heads of a Friends college."[8]

A constituent who seems to have had close ties to the college wrote President Dennis: "The father of an Earlham student and another man who attended years ago asked me what I knew about Negro boys dating white girls at the college. I knew nothing until then. I was troubled. I told them I supposed because there were fewer students this year they all felt well acquainted and didn't realize the implications. Perhaps there were not enough white boys to help the others 'know their place.' I didn't quite mean that, but that the white boys would know how to keep them straight! Well, my wife told me not to give Earlham another penny if that went on."[9]

The college was reflecting the wider society's fears, not just about race but about women too. As free as women of the twenties were, perhaps *because* they were freer, they needed protection. They were stepping out into a world whose evils their supposedly innocent minds couldn't comprehend. It was the responsibility of benevolent men to watch over them.

A CONSTRUCTION JOB in the summer of 1931 gave Daniel enough money to return to school that fall. A few changes had occurred during his absence: Student enrollment had dropped, due to the economic hardships of the time, and the college, keeping up with current educational trends, had created a Department of Psychology. That year Daniel was elected the Day Lighters' representative to the Student Senate.

He'd been studying to be a doctor, but when he began to calculate how long it would take, especially after the two-year hiatus, it seemed to a young man in his early twenties as if he'd be studying till he was quite old. He changed his major to Spanish, with the goal of teaching.

Daniel: "I don't regret it. Teaching's helped me adjust to the changing of the generations and been a way of keeping me younger. If you're not with young people, you can't understand them."

"I JUST HEARD Prex is going to call you into his office," Ned Stewart whispered in the library, his tone hinting that the visit was not going to be for purposes of friendliness or praise. Sure enough, later in the day Daniel found a note in his mailbox requesting his presence in the president's office at two o'clock the following afternoon.

It was a masculine room, with dark wood paneling, leather chairs, and an enormous oak desk. Dr. Dennis, who had come to Earlham during Daniel's two-year absence, appeared to be in his early fifties, with a wide forehead and graying hair at the temples. A graduate of Earlham just before the turn of the century, he'd spent several years as an international lawyer in

Washington D.C., returning with an urbane manner that could be rather intimidating to students from small towns and rural areas.

"Good afternoon, Mr. Winters." The president removed reading glasses perched on the end of his nose.

Daniel took a seat in a brown leather chair, mindful of sitting erect and positioning his long legs parallel, feet flat on the floor. In preparation for this meeting he'd carefully applied pomade, polished his shoes, taken extra time ironing his shirt and pressing the crease in his pants. Hands resting on the arms of the chair, he now gazed across the wide desk separating him and Dr. Dennis.

"Let me begin, Mr. Winters, by saying how proud we are to have you here at Earlham. We're happy to have such an exemplary person as you to represent your race. Your presence has done a lot for race relations here at the college."

"Thank you, sir." Daniel stiffened, suspicious that the president's affirming words were going to be followed by *but.*

"But there's a little problem." The president paused a moment to clear his throat. "We've had some complaints about you."

Daniel couldn't imagine what President Dennis might be referring to. "What kinds of complaints?"

"Well, it appears that you frequently are seen walking into town with some of the girls, and several of the town residents are complaining about that."

Daniel dug his long fingers into the arms of the chair. He knew that by *girls,* Dr. Dennis meant *white* girls. "Sir, I travel to and from school on the streetcar. When I walk into town to catch it, I don't ask those girls to go with me. They walk with me because they're going that direction, too."

"I'm certain, Mr. Winters, that your intentions toward them are not dishonorable. But young women are often naive about appearances. They tend to lack good judgment on matters related to the public's discernment of their actions. I trust you will find some way to protect them and the college from further embarrassment. I hope I have made my point. Thank you for coming." He stood. The meeting was over. It had taken no more than three minutes.

Leaving the office, Daniel fumed. Who he was supposed to walk with? Was he expected always to be alone? And did the well-to-do women who lived near the college have nothing better to do than peer from behind their lace curtains at students walking into town?

When some of the students heard about *the problem,* they told their parents. The mother of one contacted the college to say her daughter would choose her own friends, with no dictates from the college. Another's father wrote of being appalled that a Quaker school had taken a stance so blatantly contradicting the Friend's belief in the dignity of all people.

FOUNDED IN 1905, the *Chicago Defender* became the most influential black newspaper in the U.S. With more than two-thirds of its readers living outside of Chicago, it covered issues of importance to African Americans (referred to as *the Race*), such as lynching and racial inequality. Its articles and editorials contrasting life in Chicago with conditions in the South played a major role in the Great Migration, the movement that brought more than one and a half million African Americans to the North between 1915 and 1925. The newspaper also lifted up the accomplishments of black Americans, whether or not they lived in Chicago.

In a file drawer in the alcove, Daniel had a yellowed newspaper clipping from the *Chicago Defender,* Saturday, June 24, 1933, accompanied by a photo of him.

"Spanish Scholar, senior at Earlham College, a Quaker school in Richmond, Indiana. He was the first race student to be awarded the medal for excellence in Spanish, given annually by the Spanish Association of Teachers of Spanish. The medal was awarded by Mrs. Anna Stanford, professor of Spanish, during chapel hour. Besides being proficient in his studies, Winters is an all-round athlete. He resides in Richmond, Indiana, with his parents."

A similar article appeared in the *Indianapolis Recorder:* "Daniel Winters, of Richmond, Indiana, a recent June graduate of

Earlham College, proved to be a very outstanding student. Winters majored in Spanish, English, and biology. He received a medal this year given annually by the Spanish Teachers Association. Mr. Winters is the first colored student to receive it. Mr. Winters is doing his practice teaching at Crispus Attucks High School."

JUST DOWN THE road from Richmond, not more than forty miles, lies the town of Muncie. In 1929, when Daniel was twenty-one years old, a team of cultural anthropologists, led by Robert and Helen Merrell Lynd, published their study of Muncie, with the intent of developing a profile of life and attitudes in a small American city.[10] The anthropologists chose Muncie—Middletown, they called it—because it was a homogeneous community with an industrial base and few people who were foreign born or black. These criteria fit Richmond as well.

By the 1920s the lines between sub groups of Muncie were sharply drawn, and racial segregation was part of town life. School principals meeting at the Y.M.C.A. to plan intramural basketball games were told that if their team had a Negro player, the school could not play at the Y. News of interest to the black community appeared in newspaper columns labeled "In Colored Circles." Black children played in parks set aside for them.

The authors of the study spoke of the Ku Klux Klan having come into town "like a tornado" at the invitation of leading businessmen, ostensibly to clean up Democratic Party politics. By 1923 the Klan had 3,500 members in Muncie. When interest in local Democratic Party politics faded, the Klan's work switched to its national agenda: spreading hatred against Catholics, Jews, and Negroes. As Muncie businessmen drifted out of the organization, the group drew its members from the working class.

"I am a member of the Klan," one Muncie man told interviewers, "because I believe before Almighty God that it is His appointed instrument"[11]

The Lynds returned to Muncie a decade later and published their new findings in *Middletown in Transition*.[12] They found that over the ten years the division between Negroes and whites had deepened. In fact, they observed, "They (Negroes) are the most marginal population in Middletown."[13] They lived in two sections of town, one inhabited only by blacks, the other by blacks and poor whites. Streets in these sections were unpaved or poorly paved.

The new study found that working class whites in Muncie resented Negroes because they competed for the same jobs or because their neighborhoods adjoined each other. In the mid-thirties blacks could only find employment in those jobs that required hard physical labor, such as carrying hod, working on road gangs, "and, in exceptional cases where a Negro man's character is above question, as janitors."[14]

"An officer in a large automobile plant stated simply, 'We don't have any Negroes at all. It's degrading to a white man to have Negroes doing the same type of work.'"[15]

In the Lynd study we get a glimpse of why Earlham administrators steered students away from dating across color lines, why they tried to prevent dialogue about interracial marriages, why Dr. Dennis called Daniel to task just for walking with white girls. Attitudes about interracial marriage were summed up in the words of a Muncie lawyer speaking at the capitol building in Indianapolis: "Rome fell because she mixed her blood. God Almighty has commanded us, 'Thou shalt not mix thy blood.' *The Outlook*—or some other periodical—reported the other day 113 marriages last year in Boston between whites and blacks, and I'm sorry to say it was white women marrying black men. We must protect American womanhood."[16]

Chapter 5

*A*NNA HASN'T THOUGHT *about it in years: the humiliation of losing the farm, her father's conduct. She wasn't old enough to know what was going on, so it must be Violet's sense of disgrace she feels. Yet old emotions merge with newer ones, and she can't tell whether the intense hurt she now feels is related to what occurred a lifetime ago or to a more recent humiliation. Both are associated with losing something.*

After a dinner of tamales she purchased from a vendor whose food she trusts not to make a gringo sick, she and Nancy look through college photo albums. Black and white photos held onto black pages by black triangles. It doesn't seem all that long ago when that young woman in slacks with shoulder length blond hair strode down a path, her straight back and raised chin giving an air of self-confidence. Each year, when the Women's Athletic Association held Tag Day, Anna was tagged for her exemplary posture. Funny, who speaks of good posture these days?

Appearance, it's all appearance. Yes, the young woman in the photos was pretty, but only Anna has any memory of what was going on inside her mind back in those days; only she knows about the shyness and hesitancy.

In many ways she's still the same, a reserved woman who takes her time making friends. Daniel criticizes her for appearing unfriendly, for giving the message in the way she walks—her posture—that she thinks she's better that anyone else. She knows she's not.

After putting the albums away she and her guest follow the staircase, where her oil paintings hang, many of them of covered bridges copied from old postcards, though she probably could have painted them from memory. The art instructor walked by, took the brush from her hand, and retouched the landscapes to suit himself. So she doesn't know if they are his or hers.

She needed confidence, but his efforts left her feeling inadequate. She wanted to create, by herself, scenes that evoked memories of where she'd come from, who she'd been. He'd never been to Ohio or Indiana. How could he know what the bridges and landscape looked like? How could he know the images she held on to?

~~~

EVEN DURING THE worst days of the Great Depression, while Violet washed supper dishes and Anna dried or when they traveled by car into Dayton, Violet would say in passing, "When you go to college..." That Anna would attend college was never doubted; nor that she'd choose Manchester, which Violet and their parents had attended.

Manchester was, and remains, a Church of the Brethren college located in North Manchester, Indiana, a small town in the north central section of the state. The town's claim to fame is that Thomas R. Marshall, twenty-eighth vice president of the U.S., under Woodrow Wilson, was born there in 1854. Marshall is remembered by a few for saying "What this country needs is a really good five-cent cigar." The Eel River winds through town, its wide fertile plain supporting abundant crops of corn, soybeans, and wheat.

Money left by her mother's estate made it possible for Anna to enter college in the fall of 1935. After the sale of the house in New Freedom, which her mother's parents had paid for, Anna's share, five hundred dollars, had been placed in the hands of a trustee and invested in bonds. These earnings, along with what she earned assisting George at the grocery and working in the college library, paid for four years of school.

Three other girls from her church went to Manchester, as did young people she'd met at church camp and district-wide youth activities, many held at the college. The familiarity of the setting and people made this transition into adulthood more an adventure than a heart-wrenching breaking-away.

Many members of the Church of the Brethren still viewed higher education with suspicion. Based on their belief that the Bible was the primary and adequate source of all knowledge, they quoted the scripture, "Seek ye first the kingdom of God." Not that Brethren were, in that regard, different from their counterparts in small towns of the Midwest. In *Middletown in Transition* (1937) cultural anthropologists wrote that residents of Muncie, Indiana, believed too much education made a person unfit for practical life.[17]

For those Brethren parents who valued education, Manchester offered the environment they sought for their children: Christian teachers, strict curfew hours, and no worldly pleasures like dancing or drinking. But after dormitory doors were locked at night, girls gathered in each others' rooms gossiping about who had gone dancing in Ft. Wayne and returned after curfew and who had been caught taking advantage of the 1933 repeal of Prohibition.

In 1935 the college occupied slightly more than two blocks and was shaded by large oak trees. Given the economic climate in the country, there was barely enough money to pay professors and staff, much less invest in campus upkeep. Plaster fell off dormitory walls, exterior paint pealed, and it wasn't unusual for buckets to be strategically located in classrooms when it rained.

Though by the thirties many in the church had forsaken plain garb, Otho Winger, president of the college since 1911, still wore the once-obligatory black pants and jacket with a standup collar buttoned to the base of the neck. (In the 1960s a similar coat, the Nehru jacket, gained wide popularity.) To many parents Winger's presence at Manchester seemed rather like sending Grandfather along with their son or daughter to make sure Christian standards were upheld. Brother Winger not only knew everyone by name but could also in many cases cite students' ancestry.

By today's standards campus activities of the late 1930s might seem boring. On Anna's first Saturday night on campus, the junior class sponsored a treasure hunt. Piled into cars, some with rumble seats, groups of students combed the countryside searching for clues: at the cemetery, inside the piano in a music practice room, in a hole in an oak tree. Each time Anna leaned her head into the circle of teammates gathered around pieces of paper holding cryptic clues about where to go next. "Mooood. Cow?" someone said. "Something to do with cows." "Robin Hood," another student said. "Robin Hood's barn?" The next message was hidden in a college barn, where a herd of dairy cows provided milk for the campus. Her team wasn't the first to locate the treasure: a big barrel of cider hidden in a professor's barn. Ping pong, a dart-throwing tournament, anagrams, and victrola music (without dancing, of course) occupied everyone for the rest of the evening.

By 1935 student voices were beginning to be heard on Brethren college campuses. At Manchester they argued that if they were going to be required to sit in assigned seats three times a week, they deserved better chapel speakers. They also tried to convince the Board of Trustees to allow dancing. The board held its ground: definitely not.

Meanwhile the faculty complained that students were misusing the library. Many spent time there dozing; others visited. One solution: pass out *sleeping slips,* three of which would deprive transgressors of library privileges. But talking continued to be an issue. A professor was heard to say (in the library, so that many could hear him) that the library had "become a den of conversationalists, with students playing peek-a-boo around lamp shades."

Campus life wasn't entirely parochial. Compared with President Winger, the faculty of forty full-time teachers—of whom six had earned doctorates—seemed sophisticated. Dr. Andrew Cordier, a popular history professor, was involved in the League of Nations and served as a speech writer for Alf Landon, who unsuccessfully ran for President in 1936.

"War is sin," the Historic Peace Churches (which included the Brethren, Friends, and Mennonites) declared in a 1935 paper titled "Principles of Christian Peace and Patriotism." A strong peace movement was developing on campus, and later, when the U.S. became involved in World War II, Manchester pacifists had already planted the seeds for the creation of the National Service Board for Religious Objectors. Instead of serving in the military, young Brethren men would be allowed Alternative Service, such as working in mental hospitals or on construction projects.

Given the college had only seven hundred students, it was practically inevitable that when classes resumed in the fall of 1937, Anna met Inez, who had transferred from McPherson, a Brethren college in Kansas. In an interview after Anna's death, Inez attributed their becoming close friends to Anna's acute awareness of who might feel marginalized. They were also drawn together because of their goals. In contrast to most other young women, intent on finding a suitable husband and having a family,

Inez and Anna both wanted a career, Anna in social work, Inez in education.

Psychology in the late thirties was still an emerging science, and on a Brethren campus Freudian ideas, especially the human inclination toward sex and aggression, provoked controversy. *Man* had, after all, been created in God's image. Yet for a young woman forging an identity, psychology professor A.R. Eikenberry represented both a father image and a source of self-understanding. After class, in conversations with Inez, Anna probed the mysteries of who she was and why she thought as she did. If our early years influence who we become, she wondered, what was the significance of losing her mother? She didn't know what to do with her strong emotions, most of them negative, about her father. She wanted friendship and love, she told Inez, but having been abandoned in childhood she didn't ever want to be hurt like that again.

Anna wasn't going to let anyone define her, Inez later observed. Since, unlike most of the other students, she had no parents to pass on a family identity, she would decide for herself who she would be. She wasn't going to push herself on anyone either; rather she hung back, seeming to say, *Once you know me you will like me. It will take awhile, though.* And to every young man she gave a clear signal that she wasn't all that interested in a close relationship. This attitude, Inez thought, sometimes created distance between Anna and others, who interpreted her demeanor as unfriendly, aloof. Yet Inez recognized that Anna was in fact shy and not nearly as confident as outward appearances might suggest.

THE DOORS OF Oakwood Hall had been locked for the night. In a second floor room six girls gathered for a *buzz* session. These conversations had the potential of being an edifying dialogue about issues of consequence but more often turned to gossip: who Brother Winger had reprimanded for inappropriately displaying affection, what girl allowed a boy to take liberties. Anna wasn't usually included in these get-togethers. The skills of making small talk eluded her; besides, she worked long hours in the library.

But she was part of a buzz session on this particular night because Florence Baker had reached out to her, said something about her having hair like Carole Lombard, and offered to set it after curfew. Boyish styles of the twenties had been replaced with soft feminine curls produced by wrapping small strands of hair around a finger and pinning the curls to the head with bobby pins, an arm-tiring endeavor for someone doing her own. In her pajamas Anna sat cross-legged on Florence's bed, handing bobby pins back to her. On the other bed Florence's roommate deftly wrapped another girl's hair around her index finger. Two girls sat on the floor, unbraiding their shoulder-length hair then brushing it vigorously. They came from conservative families who took seriously the Apostle Paul's words, "But if a woman have long hair, it is a glory to her: for her hair is given her for a covering."

"You know," Florence's roommate said, "I'm thinking of spending—oops, sorry I poked you—I'm thinking about spending the summer in Chicago. Get a job as a nanny."

Anna had been to Indianapolis a few times, Cincinnati too. She liked cities: the smells of frying doughnuts and corndogs wafting out onto a sidewalk; the way stores, especially in the spring and summer, displayed colorful new clothing in their wide windows. Liked too the way city people walked as if they had a definite purpose, even their impatient honks and shouts. (Years of living with the grime and exhaust fumes of Mexico City later diminished her enthusiasm for urban adventure.)

She paid close attention as different girls spoke.

"Your parents must not be like mine. They'd never let me go."

"Mine either. They'd be afraid I'd get killed by gangsters."

"Or some stranger would corrupt your morals."

The conversation continued, Florence commenting on the glamour of Chicago, one of the conservative girls complaining about over-protective parents. Anna sat quietly, picturing herself, not as the small-town girl she was but as a sophisticated young woman confidently walking along State Street.

When summer came, the summer of 1938, she was one of five Manchester girls headed for Chicago.

~~~

STORYBOOKS ABOUT BEARS and little girls, walks to the park for a picnic lunch, and piggyback rides up the stairway usually seemed more like recreation than work. Anna served as upstairs maid and nanny to the Wilson's three-year-old daughter, Emily. Another woman, a permanent employee, cooked for the family and took care of the downstairs.

Sunday afternoons and all day Thursday, when they were free of work responsibilities, the five young women from Manchester College explored Chicago together, sometimes taking in a museum, more often browsing through department stores whose goods they couldn't afford. Sunday evenings they stretched out on blankets on the lawn of Grant Park, listening to free concerts.

Years later Anna laughed as she told about one of the summer's mishaps. While Mrs. Wilson and the two older girls traveled in Europe, the cook took her vacation. In everyone's absence Anna was expected to add meal preparation to her other responsibilities. On her second day as cook, Mr. Wilson called to say he was bringing another man home for dinner.

Anna felt up to the task. For the menu she would rely on the few dishes she had experience with: meatloaf and mashed potatoes. And although she'd never baked an angel food cake, it couldn't be all that different from other cakes. When dinner was served, the cohesive qualities the meatloaf lacked, the mashed potatoes had to excess. The angel food cake had gone pfft, fallen flat. Anna served the meal as though everything was as she'd intended. Mr. Wilson made not a single complaint, but he didn't invite any more dinner guests until the cook returned from vacation.

On one of her Thursdays off, as she leisurely walked through the neighborhood, she noticed a small dance studio that advertised ballroom dancing and classes in body movement. She'd grown up in a church that disapproved of dancing, a prohibition that's made many a young woman believe her body is an alien force that she must dominate rather than liberate. Fascinated by the idea of learning to respond to music in a way that felt natural, she enrolled and for the rest of the summer conscientiously attended classes. Years later she would make sure her daughters had the same opportunity.

In the minds of many Americans, Chicago's reputation was closely tied to gangsters. But those were notions left over from the previous decade, when Al Capone had amassed a fortune and spread violence. In the summer of 1938 he was still imprisoned in Alcatraz, his power diminished by the end of Prohibition. Anna and the Manchester girls moved around the city without fear.

THEIR SENIOR YEAR Inez and Anna roomed together off campus, in the home of Mrs. Leedy, who was as strict about curfew as she was about the cleanliness of her kitchen. At eleven o'clock every night Mrs. Leedy would go to the front door and turn the key, which was always in the slot, to the locked position. One night Inez wanted to spend a little extra time with her boyfriend out on the porch. She reached inside the door, removed the key from the lock, and dropped it in her coat pocket. At eleven o'clock, as she stood beside the boy in the shadows, she saw Mrs. Leedy walk toward the door then scurry about the lit parlor, no doubt in search of the key. Her conscience getting the better of her, Inez went inside and handed it to Mrs. Leedy, who wouldn't permit her to go upstairs until she'd listened to a stern lecture on honesty and morals.

Up in their room, Inez was overcome by guilt. Bemused by the whole episode, Anna couldn't understand why she took her little misdeed so seriously. "That's because you don't let anything upset you," Inez said. "All the silly campus rules, you don't like them, but you wouldn't think of breaking one. You won't even skip chapel. You know what? You're a rebel without being rebellious."

Years later, according to Inez, this statement pretty much summarized Anna's outlook.

WHAT HAD ITS origins as just another way to pass the time provided the next summer's adventure. Waiting for a friend in the lobby of a Chicago YMCA, Anna picked up a pamphlet about the College Summer Service Group in New York City. From those who applied the Y would select thirty-six college students from all over the United States to live and work in New

York for a summer. A sociology major, Anna was interested in components of the program: work experience in social service agencies and seminars in which participants could reflect on urban problems. In the spring notification of her acceptance arrived, along with a scholarship.

On May 30, 1939, the day after graduation, a friend drove her to South Bend, where she boarded an early-morning train bound for New York. She wore a pale blue suit, the skirt straight, mid-calf in length, with a slit in the back; the jacket, broad shouldered, was pulled in at the waist by a narrow belt. White gloves, a perky blue beret with a bow on the side, and open-toed navy blue shoes completed her outfit.

In movies young women rode in compartments and ate in dining cars with white linen table clothes, where they were joined by handsome men who offered them a cigarette and presented either romance or danger. Anna, who could afford no more than coach fare, certainly no meals, carried sandwiches in her purse. A man from across the aisle hoisted her cardboard suitcase onto the rack above, and she settled in by the window, intent on watching the landscape, maybe napping a little too.

Instead of a handsome stranger, a woman she guessed to be approaching fifty sat down beside her. Not a quiet woman sensitive to Anna's wish for solitude, but a loquacious one wearing a bright green hat, wide-brimmed with a cluster of velvet red flowers and a sizable yellow bird whose tail feather protruded well beyond the rim. The lady was from Chicago, on her way to New York to care for a younger sister who'd just given birth to her fifth child. Constitutionally unable to be rude, Anna listened to the women's incessant talking, turning away when she could to peer out the window.

Puffs of steam from the locomotive drifted back, rising like clouds over fertile farm land. At crossings black cars with shiny chrome grills waited, the loud clang-clang of a bell warning drivers to stay back. After each stop a steward came through to check tickets, interrupting the woman's narrative about how she and her husband made it through the most difficult period of the country's economic crisis by selling cheese or how brilliant her son was. At fifteen he resembled Clark Gable. Had Anna ever been to Chicago? Yes, she said, but the woman wasn't interested in any details.

Sixteen hours after passengers boarded, having entered New York through a long tunnel, the train emerged into Grand Central. With both hands Anna lugged her heavy suitcase down the steps of the railroad car. All around her passengers were embracing friends or family members. Searching the crowd for a placard that was supposed to greet her, she nearly ran into the man who'd lifted her suitcase up on the rack in South Bend and taken it down upon arrival in New York. He held a child in the crook of his arm while a woman—no doubt his wife—enthusiastically embraced him. Anna envied the young family.

A sign saying "Welcome, Summer Service Group" appeared as an appendage of a young man in a brown suit standing some distance away. Suitcase at her side, Anna moved toward him. He took it and led her through the cavernous concourse. She risked looking like a country bumpkin, lifting her chin to stare at the ceiling so far above, while around her scurrying people, many of them men carrying briefcases, created exhilarating confusion.

People in motion, cars in motion. Even at night nothing seemed to stand still in this city. Maneuvering his Ford through traffic, the driver tried to initiate a conversation, but Anna only responded as politely as possible without shifting her eyes from the car window. They'd probably been traveling half an hour when he stopped in front of a drab, gray building and announced, "This is it, your home for the summer."

A cooperative residence for students at New York University, the building had little in common with Oakwood Hall. Pungent, foreign smells came from the kitchen, the toilet on her floor frequently overflowed, and several times between the bathroom and her room she nearly collided with a young man returning late at night, drunk. By the end of the summer she had been invited to eat with two young women from India, mastered the plunger, and managed to avoid, more times than not, the drunken man.

It wasn't that she'd anticipated a roommate similar to Inez or that she expected to become close friends with Helen. But she was surprised when her summer roommate's first words were, "I think we should be clear with each other from the beginning. I'm a lesbian." Back at Manchester girls in the dorm had talked about lesbians, but to the best of Anna's knowledge she'd never met one.

It took some careful, deliberate thought before she was able to respond: "I don't see why that should keep us from getting along." Over the summer they had a few conversations, but Helen's time was filled with her studies, and the Summer Service Group took nearly all of Anna's days and evenings.

Each member of the Summer Service Group worked thirty hours a week for a social service agency, Anna for a child-care facility. Monday and Wednesday afternoons were set aside for seminars and tours of agencies. Program participants visited all parts of the city, studying the social conditions and meeting political, cultural, and educational leaders. They met in seminars with Mayor LaGuardia, controversial liberal pastor and radio preacher Harry Emerson Fosdick, Wall Street bankers, and the president of the Real Estate Board of New York. Small groups investigated housing, sanitation, city politics, and race relations. Saturdays and Sundays everyone explored points of interest, such as Greenwich Village, Chinatown, and Harlem.

Harlem was like nothing Anna had ever seen—Negro women sitting out on stoops with baby carriages and calling to each other; people leaning out of windows; beautiful friezes around doors and windows. By this time the Great Depression had taken its toll. The night clubs of the twenties, where black performers had entertained white audiences and a black middle class had flourished, were closed. The area now suffered from high unemployment and poverty.

Most of the literary figures of the Harlem Renaissance had moved on, but painting and sculpture were thriving. The group spent an entire afternoon in the studio of sculptor Augusta Savage, a warm, magnetic person, known not only as an artist but as a woman committed to helping young black artists. Anna particularly admired one of Savage's works: a small cluster of people within the palm of a hand. It cost ten dollars, too expensive for a young woman fresh out of college with no job.

Sunday evenings were devoted to group building and sharing the week's experiences. Looking around the room on one of the last Sundays of the summer, Anna marveled at how her world had grown. Not only had this trip to New York broadened her understanding of social problems, it also offered an opportunity she'd never had before: the chance to develop relationships with people from different racial, ethnic, and class backgrounds.

Anna: "The Y's summer service program was a wonderful experience and crystallized the values I'd grown up with. This was an idealistic group, and everything we did focused on improving social conditions and relationships between people."

MOVIES OF THE thirties inevitably depicted black women and men as servants. Louise Beavers was a perennial combination maid/mammy, a black woman who had to practice the illiterate sounding dialect whites associated with blacks, and had to eat more than she wanted to maintain the rotund figure a black maid *should* have. Her feigned stupidity made Mae West appear all the more savvy. Black male actors, such as Stepin Fetchit, entertained white audiences with a slow shuffle, a childlike nature, and a lack of intelligence.

The Du Sable Museum of African American History in Chicago exhibits advertising that depicted blacks. There was one for Nigger Hair Tobacco, which showed a black man with a big ring in his nose; an ad for Fern Glen Rye, in which a black man stood in the road, a turkey in one hand, a watermelon in the other, looking down at a bottle of Fern Glen lying in the middle of the road. "I'se in a perdickermunt," the caption said.

In the kitchens of friends Anna would probably have seen salt and pepper shakers in the shape of black children, hair standing up, whites of their eyes wide with fright. Aunt Jemima spice containers and cookie jars could be found practically everywhere. Perhaps Violet and George, when they returned from waiting tables in Florida, brought home a coconut painted to look like the caricature of a black woman, with wide white eyes and big red lips, "Souvenir of Florida" written on the back.

During that summer in New York Anna noticed the contrast between such caricatures—the buffoons, the docile servants—and the Negroes with whom she came into contact each day.

STANDING ALONG THE edge of the narrow road, hands on hips, Anna stared at her car. Her '36 Chevy coup was down in the ditch. On its side. She looked out over the flat Indiana farmland, fields of brown stalks of corn ready for harvest, but saw no other cars. She reached into her purse for a handkerchief, gently whisking it across the front of her navy blue slacks, brushing off smudges of dust picked up from climbing out the car window and over the running board. A barely audible laugh escaped her throat as she thought about that morning—the excitement of embarking on yet another adventure. She was on her own, with a job, a car, and a future that was hers to create. But those had been morning thoughts, musings yet untested by the day's realities.

It hadn't been easy finding a job. Ironically, the only ones were those that helped people who didn't have jobs. Finally hired by the State Unemployment Relief Commission, she had just completed a month's training in Indianapolis and was on her way to a new position in the Gary office. Since her responsibilities would involve traveling all over northern Indiana, a car was essential. She and George had spent Saturday searching until they came across this one. The 350 dollars seemed expensive for a young woman fresh out of college, but George thought it a good enough deal to warrant lending her the money.

She'd only had time for four hours of driving instruction. On country roads, with George on the other end of the bench seat, she learned to shift gears—lurching forward, then stalling, starting again, lurching again. Maybe if there'd been more time to practice, she wouldn't have lost control when the tire blew out. She wouldn't be standing by a ditch, gazing down at her car resting on its side.

The chug of a tractor drew her attention. A middle-aged farmer in bib overalls jumped down and after saying something about *a maiden in distress,* walked over to the car. Planting both feet firmly on the ground, he used the weight of his body to pull on the elevated end of the bumper. The car began to rock, gently at first, until the arc of its swing became large enough that one immense exertion of strength accompanied by a wretched moan allowed gravity to take over. The wheels that had been in the air bounced on the ground. Connecting car and tractor with a rope and instructing Anna to return to the driver's seat, the farmer eased her Chevy out of the ditch. He changed the tire, and she was back on her way to adventure.

IN SPITE OF two summers spent sampling urban life in Chicago and New York City, Anna recognized she was far from worldly wise. Her curiosity about places and people led her, at age twenty-one, to make a conscious decision: In her foray into career and adult life she would not let the rules of the church constrain her but would be guided by common sense.

The church censured dancing, yet on that summer day in Chicago she'd determined for herself that moving in time to music might even be wholesome. The church denounced drinking alcoholic beverages, yet the new friends she made on her first job in Gary enjoyed going out together for drinks.

Not usually shocked by life outside the protective communities in which she'd grown up and gone to college, she quickly discovered, though, that her inexperience could place her in uncomfortable situations.

ALL HER CAR needed were a few adjustments the morning she and Madeleine took it to the garage. As young social workers assigned to the Gary office, the two shared a room—with kitchen privileges and a bathroom down the hall—in the Victorian home of a Methodist minister. Madeleine was engaged to be married, but after only a few months of knowing her, Anna couldn't help but notice the attention her roommate gave men, attention that was always reciprocated.

The linoleum floor of the garage waiting room looked as if it hadn't been mopped in years. While Anna took a seat in one of four chairs with metal arms and grimy red plastic seat covers, Madeleine stepped up to the counter. Apparently she didn't mind that its surface was no cleaner than the floor, for she rested an elbow on it and gazed flirtatiously into the eyes of Weldon, the owner. Tossing her head back in laughter, thrusting her bountiful bosom forward as she tilted her chin, she advertised sexual energy.

"How about going into Chicago sometime?" Weldon asked. "To a movie, say."

Madeleine nodded toward Anna. "If you'll bring somebody along for her."

"I'm not interested," Anna said from the chair.

Madeleine arched her eyebrows and leaned closer to Weldon. "If you want me, you'll have to convince her."

"Frank," Weldon called toward the garage, "come out from under there a minute." From beyond the waiting room could be heard the clang of a metal tool being dropped on a cement floor. "What's your name, Sweetheart?" Weldon asked.

"Anna," she replied coolly.

The man who entered the waiting room reminded her a little of Jimmy Stewart, dark hair slicked back, earnest eyes, a diffident smile. "Frank," Weldon said, "I want you to meet Anna. Anna, this is Frank."

Frank stepped over to where Anna sat, wiped his hand on his overalls, and extended it. "Hello," was all he said.

"Anna," Weldon said from behind the counter, "how could you turn down the opportunity to go to a show with this man? Sure, he's got grease under his fingernails, but that grease is a symbol all over this country of men who work hard for a living and deserve a little fun with a pretty girl."

Weldon and Frank did seem to be good-natured, so in spite of her apprehension about going out with strangers, she agreed to be Frank's date. Seated in a Chicago movie theater the next night, she concluded she had nothing to fear.

After the movie they drove a short distance to a hotel, where Anna assumed they were going to dance. Instead, Weldon and Frank, hands clasping their dates' elbows, steered them into the hotel lobby. Anna began to feel nervous.

Weldon motioned the women to wait by a large pillar. "We'll be right back," he said.

He and Frank approached the marble hotel desk. Anna moved closer to Madeleine. "What did you get me into?" she whispered.

Madeleine stepped away, ostensibly to examine a mural on the wall, leaving Anna to stand by the pillar, feet firmly planted, arms folded around her purse. Weldon returned to Madeleine and, his arm at her waist, guided her toward the elevator. Seconds later Frank stood beside Anna. He reached for her hand. She pulled it away.

"I'm sorry, Frank, but I came into town for a show and perhaps some dancing, not for anything more." Obviously surprised, he remained polite, taking her to dance in the lounge while Madeleine and Weldon were upstairs.

Back in their room, Anna confronted Madeleine. "You knew exactly what was going to happen, that we were all going to end up at the hotel, but you didn't tell me."

"You're a big girl. I assumed you wouldn't think it was any big deal."

"You mean you assumed I was just like you are."

"Don't make it sound as though I go to bed with every man I meet."

Anna resisted the impulse to say that it certainly appeared that way. Instead she asked, "What kind of a relationship do you have with Allen, that you can be engaged yet go out with other men? I'd think if you loved him enough to marry him, you wouldn't find other men so hard to resist."

"You miss the point. I want to get all this out of my system. Before I get married."

"Oh. So you think there is something *in your system* that craves the attention of every man you meet. And at that moment when Allen slips the ring on your finger this thing *in your system* will suddenly disappear because you've got it *out of your system?*"

For a moment Madeleine just stood and stared at her roommate. "It's clear," she finally said, "that you don't understand the difference between sex and love."

Anna: "I could have found myself in a dangerous situation. I had this idea I could take care of myself, though, and it never let me down. I got into a few difficult spots, but I got out of them without getting panicky. Almost instinctively, you might say, I discovered that if I acted as though I had the situation under control, I gained control."

"BLESSED BE THE tie that binds our hearts in Christian love," Anna had often sung at church. Yet once she graduated from college she no longer felt bound to the Church of the Brethren. She had Violet and George and a small circle of friends, but no group of people concerned about her wellbeing. She was alone in the world, and getting through life was going to require emotional strength and keen interpersonal perception. Without anyone to protect her, she would have to protect herself. Without anyone to nurture her, she would have to find nurture within herself.

Chapter 6

*S*ITTING IN FRONT *of the fireplace drinking daiquiris with Daniel and Nancy, Anna considers how over the years she's often wished for this kind of evening, where the warmth of the room blends with the warmth of friendship. Daniel isn't usually this comfortable with her friends.*

He puts down his drink and leans forward. "Why did you marry your husband?" he asks Nancy.

She gives the question some thought. "Maybe because he was the opposite of my father. With direction and drive. Strength of character too, which I admired."

She turns to Anna. "Why did you marry Daniel?" she asks.

Anna doesn't hesitate. "He excited me!" Nancy made a rational choice, she thinks. I did not. I got the flame, she the lasting embers.

There's a long period of silence. The conversation of the past few days has been so continuous that the clock's ticking drew no attention. Now its rhythmic beat fills the room. In this silence Anna wonders what the clock speaks of. Of time that has passed or time that is passing? When did it start ticking away minutes, hours, that could no longer be shared?

Now, as she and Daniel sit here, at ages sixty-nine and seventy-eight, she wonders how much time they have to continue the arduous task of reviving their marriage.

LATE 1940. ANNA had a new job: supervisor of an office of the State Unemployment Relief Commission. In a new location: Richmond, Indiana. She looked forward to living near Violet and family, now making their home in Richmond. Violet and George had two daughters, Joyce and Myra.

The Unemployment Relief office was located in the same brick building as the local Works Progress Administration, where a tall, slender Negro man with the hint of a receding hairline spent his days. Evenings he taught a Spanish class for adults. His name was Daniel Winters. Because he was a sociable type, with not enough to keep him busy in the WPA office, he frequently sauntered down the wide wooden staircase to chat with the young women at Anna's agency.

Daniel: "Several women worked there, but there was something about one in particular that I especially found attractive. I liked the way she carried herself, the way she held her head high. There was a touch of reserve, but it was a reserve of warmth not of coolness. I used to see Anna walking into the building—she had a *very* nice figure. Oh, boy, how she came into that building. I still like to watch her walk. For several years now she's had to leave before me in the morning, and after she closes the door, I go to the window and open the curtains just to watch her walk down the street and turn the corner."

In spite of a shapely body, a complexion as smooth as any in make-up ads, and blond hair that rested in gentle waves on her shoulders—features one might have expected to render a woman confident—Anna tended to feel awkward around men. But Daniel had a way about him, a social grace some consider charm. His dark eyes conveyed sincerity. His intellect and facility with conversation put others at ease. And when he flashed that wide grin…

Anna: "I don't know when we began to talk, but we had some interesting conversations, and he fascinated me as a person. Color—that wasn't an issue. Of course, I wasn't thinking of *marrying* him!"

SHE WAS MERELY going to watch a man teach Spanish, Anna reminded herself as she removed one dress at a time from the narrow closet, held it up for inspection, put it back. He had come downstairs from the WPA office and stood by her desk, his dark eyes flickering with an affability that made her forget she was shy.

"You've asked me about my teaching philosophy," he'd said. "Why don't you come see for yourself? Tonight." Out of politeness—that's all the invitation had been, a polite gesture. And she was responding with friendliness.

She finally settled on a dress of turquoise wool, more stylish than her other clothes, with ample shoulder pads and a flattering gored skirt. A comb through her shoulder-length blond hair, a dab of lipstick on each cheek to add color, a glance in the mirror to make sure her stocking seams were straight, and she was ready to go.

A light snow began to fall as she drove her '36 Chevy coup to the high school where adult classes met in the evening hours.

Watching him from the back of the room, she found this Daniel Winters even more compelling than at the office. In his teaching he had a self-confidence and dynamism she hadn't seen in many men. Students, all of them white, actively participated as Daniel led them through Spanish verb tenses.

When the class ended, she remained seated as men and women drifted out of the room. Gathering his papers and books, Daniel paused to look over at her, flashing a smile that made her heart lurch. For fear she was blushing, she turned away slightly.

"I assume you drove," he said.

"Yes."

"How about if we drive around for a while?"

Minutes later, Daniel behind the wheel of her car, they talked about the U.S. economy and tensions in Europe. He pulled the car to the curb and turned off the engine. Soon snow clung to the windows, diffusing the glow of the nearby street light, hiding the houses beyond the sidewalk. Insulated from the outside world, their vulnerabilities protected from its harshness, they began to speak of personal matters. Anna found herself telling him about feeling abandoned through much of her childhood, how her sister and brother-in-law had included her in their family.

Though at work Daniel exuded self-confidence, it was a different voice she heard as they sat in their cocoon, his words spoken so softly she had to strain to hear. With a tremor in his voice, he talked about his love of sports and how, because he was a Negro, his playing opportunities had been limited. He told about another night when the snow was falling, being barred from a YMCA locker room while his white teammates went in to change, how lonely his young self had felt.

She was the one who finally had to remind them both that tomorrow was a work day. Daniel shifted his body and started the engine. With his handkerchief he wiped away the fog that had gathered on the inside of the window and turned on the wipers to brush away the snow. As he leaned back, waiting for the windshield to clear, he rested his arm on the seat behind her. Slowly he let it drop to her shoulder, then pulling her toward him, he kissed her.

It was a gentle kiss, wonderfully tender. The meeting of their lips, one of his hands resting ever so lightly at her waist, the other pulling her toward him—even through her heavy winter coat, her body was sensitive to every place he touched her.

Their lips parted; his hands returned to the steering wheel; the car moved forward. They rode in silence until Daniel asked, "Are you sorry I kissed you?"

"I'd rather you hadn't." Which wasn't exactly the truth, for the single kiss had stirred a desire for more. On the other hand it *was* the truth. This wasn't the right man.

WITH EVERYONE ELSE gone home, Anna was completing the week's paper work when Daniel entered the office. He walked over to the oak file cabinet next to her desk, rested his arm on top of it. The nature of their conversations had changed since the night she'd gone to see him teach. Since the kiss.

"I'd like to see you again," he said. "How about if we take a long drive Sunday afternoon?"

"I'd like that very much."

"I CAN GET you on at Harvester," Daniel's friend Carl Henderson told him in early 1941. Formed in 1902 by J.P. Morgan, International Harvester manufactured farm equipment and played an important role in Richmond's economy. "They've got an opening for a janitor. Doesn't pay much, but it's probably better than what you're getting over at the WPA." He was right. It did pay a little more: fifteen cents an hour.

Asserting that Negroes were intellectually incapable of operating complicated machinery, management only hired them to clean the shop or shovel coal outside. Six days a week Daniel gathered machine shavings, shoveled them into a cart, and delivered them to the Salvage Department for later use.

Though his new job left him exhausted, he managed to wash off the grime and meet Anna a night or two a week. Unable to court publicly, they talked and kissed and held each other in the privacy of her black Chevy coup. This was necessary for two reasons: First, heads would turn if a biracial couple appeared along the streets of Richmond.

Second, Daniel was married, the father of three children.

NOT UNTIL LATE in the interview did Daniel mention his first marriage, and then it was in passing, as if the topic should warrant no further discussion. Clearly he wanted only to talk about his growing up with racism, his love for Anna. He was agitated by questions about his first marriage.

Had I been a journalist I probably would have probed more, but I was a guest in their home, there because of my relationship to Anna through Violet, and it was obvious from our first day that Daniel had been reluctant to undertake this project. So I left Mexico City with scant information about his relationship with Martha, his first wife.

He was vague about dates. But once I began adding and subtracting, it became evident that he was still married when his and Anna's romance began. I later learned from talking with Carl Henderson that in the early days of unionizing the Harvester plant, workers met in Daniel's and Martha's front parlor. Even if he didn't tell Anna in the beginning, she had to have suspected, given his age, that he was married.

Anna quit following all the church's rules, she said, but given her religious upbringing, I can't help but believe she lost sleep over this relationship. I imagine her breaking it off more than once, being angry at Daniel for his lack of forthrightness, then telling herself, as many women have, *But I love him.*

And there was the issue of Daniel's three children. Abandoned by her own father to fend for herself, she surely wouldn't have wanted to feel responsible for Daniel leaving his family.

After disclosing his previous marriage in the interview, he did, however, fill in a few blanks—like what he did between the time he graduated from college in 1933 and when he met Anna in 1940.

EARLHAM HAD OFFERED Daniel few opportunities for social interaction. As a commuting student, though, he'd been able to keep up relationships with his Negro peers in town. He met Martha, one of the most sought after Negro girls around, at the roller skating rink and dated her for two years.

Two weeks after he graduated from college, they married and moved in with her mother. 1933 was a bad year for many Americans, especially a young black man looking for a job. Daniel wanted to teach, but teaching jobs were scarce. Negroes were only hired in the segregated schools of the South or in cities, such as Indianapolis, in the few schools with all-Negro student bodies. The birth of their first son, Daniel Junior, was a sharp reminder of what a man was supposed to do: provide shelter and put food on the table. What kind of man lived off his mother-in-law?

His cousin Arthur, who worked for the Chicago Police Department, wrote that he could get him a job with the department. Not an easy choice: in Richmond, week-by-week employment bringing in too little money to support them, but with a place to live; or a job in the crime-ridden Windy City, where they'd have to pay rent. After hours of discussion they decided Daniel would head for Chicago alone. Martha and little Daniel, now a month old, would join him after he'd completed training and found a place to live.

Arriving by bus at four o'clock on a Monday afternoon, carrying a cardboard suitcase held together by an old belt, Daniel headed for the apartment where Arthur and his wife lived. When a knock on the door brought no answer—strange, given they were expecting him—he sat down on the floor, leaned against the wall, and fell asleep. He awoke to see street lights' glow against the night sky. He picked up his suitcase and headed for the drugstore he'd noticed on his way. From the pay phone he tried calling Arthur at work.

"May I speak with Arthur Johnson?" he asked.

After putting him on hold for a long time, the receptionist's voice returned and said, in what seemed a strained tone, "I'm sorry, Officer Johnson can't be reached at the moment." Click.

For several minutes Daniel stood in the booth staring at the telephone as if expecting it to ring, for someone's voice to tell him what was going on. He didn't have money for a hotel and the idea of spending the night in Chicago's downtown bus station, at least fifteen blocks away, didn't appeal to him. And where was Arthur's wife, Lucy? He decided to return to their apartment and wait for someone to show up. Catch some sleep if he could.

At about ten o'clock he was again leaning against the wall of the hallway, legs stretched out on the floor in front of him. He was roused from a light sleep by the sound of a woman coming up the stairs, keys jingling in her hand. She stopped abruptly when she saw him. "Who are you" she asked. "What are you doing here?"

"I'm Daniel Winters. I'm waiting for my cousin, who lives here."

"Is your cousin named Arthur?"

"Yes."

"I'm Jasmine Hammer, a close friend of Arthur's and Lucy's." Her eyes welled with tears. "Arthur was shot and killed today while on duty." She paused to collect herself. "Lucy's spending the night at my house. I came to pick up a few things for her."

For Daniel it was a double blow: the loss of a cousin he'd been close to since childhood and the loss of a job he'd been counting on.

Fortunately Prohibition, in effect for nearly fourteen years, had ended eight months earlier. The Silver Star Café, on Chicago's Southside needed a bartender, a job Daniel knew nothing about. Not that he and his friends had complied with the Volstead Act. Neighborhood parties had simply traded beer kegs of the pre-Prohibition era for various forms of home brew, usually made from dandelions, grapes, or corn.

The walls of the lounge were covered in blue velvet sprinkled with clusters of small silver stars. Small stars also twinkled from the dark blue ceiling. Behind the bar a full length mirror repeated dazzling patterns created by the lights from walls and ceiling. The building was rumored to have once belonged to Al Capone. Still, the lounge was a respectable place, where people came for drinks and entertainment. At four in the afternoon there was a women's cocktail hour, when women could come in alone or in pairs. The occasional man who wandered in was made to know he was unwelcome. Evenings, couples, most of them black, came for live music and floor shows. It was a time of big bands.

The serious drinker who came alone would sit at the bar, in front of the big mirror, and unload his problems while Daniel cleaned up around him. Daniel looked back on his year in Chicago as an education in psychology.

THE BOXER JOE LEWIS, who had been getting a lot of attention in his amateur career, would be fighting his first professional fight at Bacon Casino, at 49th and Wabash. Daniel decided to go. Rain threatened, so he took along his raincoat. After the announcer introduced the fighters, Daniel turned his back to the ring to fold his coat so he could sit on it and be more comfortable. By the time he turned around, the referee was holding up Joe Lewis's hand. He'd already knocked out Jack Kracken. The seventy-five cents spent on an admission ticket had been wasted.

Daniel: "During the 30s nobody lifted our spirits like Joe Lewis. Those were the depression years, and Negroes suffered the hardships more than other groups in America. Into this low came the Brown Bomber. He was our hero, our champion, one of us. His potential and hard work came together in triumph, which I guess you could say we all dreamed of for ourselves."

A week after John Dillinger was shot exiting the Biograph Theater, Martha stepped off the train in Chicago. In one arm she carried Daniel Junior, in the other a suitcase.

While they waited beside interlaced streetcar tracks heading in multiple directions, Daniel tried to soften the disappointment she was sure to feel once she saw where they'd be living.

"It's not the Ritz. It's on the fourth floor and there's noise at night, and somebody—I think it's the guy three doors down—he doesn't bother to clean up after himself in the bathroom. I swear, all these people coming up here from the South. I don't think some of them are used to indoor plumbing."

Martha leaned into him. "At least we'll be together. That's what's important."

But he could tell as they stood just inside the apartment door that she was disappointed. "I promise," he said, "we'll find a better place."

IT WAS A way to escape the oppressive summer heat. Take little Daniel for an evening walk, go see where her husband tended bar. But just as Martha stepped inside the Silver Star Café, a white woman grabbed her and pushed her into an office.

"Stay here," the woman ordered.

Moments later, from the other side of the door, came sounds of gunshots, smashing glass, and shouts. More than thirty minutes passed before the woman returned and led the trembling Martha, her arms still protectively holding tight to her baby, out of the office. The mirror that ran the length of the bar was shattered.

Gladys, the owner's wife, had an instinct about danger. Her husband had been in the business long enough that she'd seen drunks, gangsters, and seemingly quiet men loosen civilizing constraints. Just moments before Martha had come on the scene, a customer had started raving that his Mexican girlfriend had stood him up. Immediately noticing that Martha was fair and might be mistaken for a Mexican, Gladys had shoved her out of sight. While Daniel crouched behind the bar, the man vented his rage as he might have done in the days of the Wild West.

After a year the couple decided Chicago was not their kind of town. Concerned about the health of Daniel's mother, now a widow, they moved back to Richmond, where they lived with her. Martha's mother died two years later, and they moved into her former home.

Theater was an interest the young couple shared. Martha had a clear, well modulated voice, and Daniel was comfortable before an audience. They performed in plays at the Thornton Center and were active for a while in Richmond's Civic Theater. At the

Civic Theater, however, they only got parts when the script called for a servant. One play in which they had small speaking roles as the maid and the butler was directed by a Mr. Halderman who kept shouting to them, "Speak like your people!"

Martha got indignant. "I am speaking like my people—plain English!" Between rehearsals they practiced together, trying to pronounce words the way Mr. Halderman wanted them to. Still dissatisfied, he replaced them both and their involvement in the Civic Theater ended.

Daniel and Martha had three children—Daniel, Emma, and Marshall. It seemed every black couple in Richmond had a son named Randall, after the community's popular black physician. They wanted their sons to someday be doctors too. Daniel and Martha agreed that since there were already too many Randalls around, they would name their second son after the doctor's brother, Marshall.

After eleven years Daniel's and Martha's marriage ended in divorce. Over the years they maintained contact, and whenever he traveled to the States, he stopped by to see her.

ANNA'S WHOLE BODY ached, and to merely lift an arm or leg required more effort than she could muster. Having survived the earlier chills and sweats, she'd now settled into a misery whose epicenter was a raw, swollen throat.

In spite of exposing the girls, Violet insisted on her moving into the small front room turned temporarily into an infirmary. Eyes drooping feverishly, hair disheveled, Anna entered her sister's house, staggered to the roll-away bed sandwiched between desk and piano, and settled into being taken care of. At times like this a big sister's doting was far more precious than independence.

By mid 1941, Anna's relationship with Daniel had progressed quickly, and the four days since she'd seen him seemed endless. He'd called only minutes before Violet came to get her, and she'd been able to tell him in a raspy voice where she would be. But given the nature of their relationship, he couldn't call or visit. Violet didn't even know he existed, and for the time being Anna wanted to keep it that way.

"Ah, ah, the patient has not been drinking her liquid," Violet scolded. "Here," she said, putting her hand beneath Anna's head and lifting it. The glass raised to her mouth was not an offering but a command.

The juice might as well have been battery fluid, it burned so intensely. Anna kept shaking her head and keeping her lips pursed. After Violet relented and left the room, Anna wasn't sure what was real and what was delirium brought on by a high fever: a whistler outside, a song only she and composer Winters knew. "You are my heavenly dream," he'd often sung to her. Briefly she thought he was in the room, holding her in his arms, stroking her hair.

Two days later she was feeling well enough to have spent part of the morning reading in bed. Violet bustled in. "Here's a letter for *you*," she chirped, tossing an envelope on the bed. Recognizing Daniel's writing, Anna simply held the letter, waiting for Violet to leave. But Violet bustled around the crowded room, adjusting a photo of the girls on top of the piano, rearranging papers on the desk. "Well, aren't you going to see who it's from?" she finally asked.

Anna slowly opened the envelope and unfolded the letter. "It's from a couple of the girls at the office. I wonder how they found out I was here."

"Well, aren't you going to read it?"

Refolding it, Anna placed her head back against the pillow and shut her eyes as though tired. "In a little bit." Her voice was weak.

She waited several minutes until Violet could be heard humming in the kitchen.

"Darling," she read. "I know it's just been a few days, yet it seems like months since I've seen you. I'm so happy when I see your face light up, but for now I must be contented with memories of it. I see so many faces, but none of them is you. I hear so many voices, but none of them is yours.

"Last night I came as near to you as I could. The light in what I think was your room was burning, and the window appeared open. My heart sat on your window ledge. Surely my love drifted through your open window. Did you know I wanted so much to come in to hold your hand and to feel the touch of my lips on yours? If I could have only said, 'Hello, Darling.'

"I've had some wild ideas—coming into your room through the window, sitting on your window sill and reading you to sleep, then kissing you nightie-night as I tucked you in. How happy I would be just to watch you sleep.

"*Yo te amo.* Daniel."

The letter remained among Anna's memorabilia.

Before the United States joined hostilities that would be called World War II, American manufacturers were producing military equipment for Great Britain, China, and the Soviet Union. As one of the companies to take on military contracts, International Harvester was forced to abide by Roosevelt's Executive Order 8802, issued June 25, 1941: "There shall be no discrimination in the employment of workers in defense industries or government because of race, creed, color, or national origin." No longer allowed to limit Negro men and women to shoveling coal and janitorial responsibilities, Harvester had no choice but to employ them in the machine shop. Finally Daniel was permitted to work there, first at a lathe, then on gear hobs.

War production also affected Anna's employment. With the creation of new jobs and an improved economy, there was no further need for the State Unemployment Relief Commission. In 1942 the state closed the Richmond offices. Anna and some of her colleagues were assigned jobs as consultants for the Indiana Public Welfare Department. She worried about what the transfer would do to her relationship with Daniel.

Along with two other young women, Dorothy and Hazel, she worked out of the regional office in Rochester, a small town in northern Indiana. A public assistance consultant, she helped local offices reorganize to meet the needs of people who couldn't work because of disabilities. Dorothy worked as a consultant for child welfare, Hazel as district representative.

They shared a four bedroom house and, despite a twelve-year age span, discovered a special compatibility. Hazel taught Anna to knit, Dorothy taught Hazel how to do calligraphy, and Anna taught Dorothy how to drive. Because of the war, butter, coffee, meat, and shoes were scarce and rationed by the government. The three women pooled their creative and financial resources so that none felt deprived. The relationships that began in that household survived more than forty-five years, and Dorothy, who once visited Daniel and Anna in Mexico, later wrote how much she treasured their friendship.

The living arrangement didn't last long, however. Hazel was devastated when the man she loved broke off the relationship. Seeking an escape, she decided to help the war effort by joining the Red Cross. This left Dorothy and Anna with more house than they needed and one fewer person to share the expenses. Anna's cousin Velma, who was married and had a baby, lived in Logansport, about twenty-five miles from Rochester. When her husband was drafted into the army, she invited Anna to live with her.

WHILE LITTLE BEATRICE tried to feed her doll a piece of toast, Anna and Velma, still in their robes, sipped coffee and shared the Saturday morning newspaper.

Velma leaned across the table, pointing to an ad. "Look. Each Wiebolt's store will award a hundred dollar savings bond to the woman with the best looking legs."

In 1940 women had rushed to buy an article of clothing that had just come out: nylon stockings. They flattered a woman's legs and didn't bunch like rayon. But with American involvement in World War II, nylon was needed for parachutes and tents. Stockings had become quite expensive and nearly impossible to find. Wiebolt's, a Chicago department store, was promoting a brand of leg makeup that offered the stocking look.

"You've got to do it," Velma said.

"Do what?"

"You've got great—if you'll furnish the legs…" She rose and walked over to the nearby bookcase, removing her Kodak Brownie from the top shelf. "I'll take the pictures and submit them."

Anna opened the bottom of her robe enough to reveal a thigh. She extended her leg and pointed her toes. Decent enough but certainly not the kind to win a contest. "It's one thing to wear shorts around the house in the summertime, quite another to display my legs to strangers."

"The judges don't know you from the man in the moon. A hundred dollars, Anna, a hundred dollars. I told you, I'll do all the work."

"There's no way I'll win."

But to placate her cousin she went to her room and put on a pair of shorts. Velma pointed her little camera, pushed the button, turned the knob that moved the film to the next unexposed frame, clicked again. As soon as the developed pictures came back, she put the best one in the mail.

Several months passed. Anna had forgotten about the contest. One evening when she returned from work, Velma met her at the door, waving an envelope from Wiebolt's.

"Open it, open it."

Anna slowly and methodically removed the letter from the envelope.

"Dear Miss Harley," she read slowly.

"Yes, yes, come on. What does it say?"

Anna looked up and grinned. "Congratulations. You have won a $100 savings bond for your entry in our recent contest."

The following week they packed Beatrice in the car and drove into Chicago to get the bond. Anna's wish for anonymity didn't work out. Along with winners from other stores, her picture was featured in Wiebolt's ad in the *Chicago Tribune*.

IT WAS A Friday evening, at the conclusion of a training conference in Indianapolis for social workers employed by the state. A group from the conference, all of them young women, sat around a restaurant table. The lights were dim; there was wine, a lot of laughter. Someone complained about the shortage of men, with the war going on.

"My cousin," one woman said, "she started writing to this man in Pennsylvania. A farmer, which is why he isn't fighting. He proposed. She accepted without ever meeting him."

"I think we're supposed to be desperate," another said. "My father's started referring to me as an old maid."

"That's cruel."

"If he doesn't stop, I might up and marry me a Negro."

"You wouldn't."

"No, you're right. I wouldn't."

Everyone giggled.

Anna sat silently sipping her wine as the discussion moved to who would and who wouldn't marry a Negro. All the other women agreed they would never marry a man of another race.

Anna put down her wine glass, dabbed her mouth with a napkin, and cleared her throat. "If you accept people as people, not according to race or class, you'd have to be open to dating a Negro, maybe marrying him."

"So would *you* date one?" The question, directed to her, was more a challenge than a request for clarification.

"If he was the kind of man I'm attracted to," she answered.

In fact, at that very moment Daniel was on his way to meet her in Indianapolis.

Chapter 7

*H*ANGING LAUNDRY, PLAYING *children, and plants profuse with bright red and pink blossoms fill roof tops up and down the street. Day and night people pass by the Winters' home, inches from the living room window, on their way to the super market at one end of the block or to the bus stop or bank on the busy street in the other direction. After thirty years, the sights, smells, and sounds of Mexico City are familiar to Anna. Yet this still doesn't feel like home.*

The conversations of the past days have reminded her that it could have been different. After their move here she not only needed Daniel's personal affirmation, but she needed him as a link to the Mexican people as well.

He's speaking now of his appreciation for self-reliant women. His mother's independent spirit probably made him more comfortable with women who show the same quality, Anna thinks but does not say. A self-reliant mother or wife seems, on the surface, to need nothing from the man. She will take care of herself, and he'll take care of himself. Her going her way frees him to go his. Why can't a man see that even the most autonomous woman sometimes needs someone to lean on? Or could it be that self-reliant women don't know how to express their needs? Leaving their husbands to assume they have none.

But the desire to take care of another eventually emerges in a man. When that occurs, he falsely assumes he has nothing to offer the independent woman. So he moves toward one who obviously needs him.

I Miss You
> From afar, traversing the many long miles
> I see your face and the loveliness of your smiles
> Brightened, lightened by the silvery moon
> On a summer night, maybe one in June.

> The pathway of the moon came slowly down
> Carrying silver dust for your fair crown
> And like the dew on the flowers' bed
> Sprinkled moon beams on your pretty head.

The light of the moon shined in your eyes
Yet the reflection I saw was not of the skies
But the beauty and depth and sweetness of love
In the soft moon glow from high above.

I bent and kissed your lips so sweet
And held you close as if to keep
That love, that memory, that night of bliss
Oh Darling, my Darling, it's you I miss.

D. W. (among Anna's mementos)

During 1943 and 1944, Anna's job brought her every two or three months from northern Indiana to meetings in Indianapolis, and nearer Daniel. In poorly lit conference rooms, a cloud of cigarette smoke hovering overhead, she feigned paying close attention as women's voices in the background ironed out problems related to new policies and how to enforce state regulations.

Elbows resting on the table, hands clasped beneath her chin, she pictured that evening's reunion with Daniel. Once he got off work he would catch a bus to Indianapolis. (The rationing of gas during wartime prohibited non-essential travel by car.) She thought about the private world the two of them had created. Alone together, holding each other close, they invited the other into that small sphere of the heart where few are welcome. He spoke of his desire to tell friends and family about their relationship; she wanted to hold it close and protect it.

That evening, when she finally saw him in the crowded bus terminal, where he was taller than everyone around him, their gazes locked. Glee Face, he called her, because her face lit up when she saw him. Two Black Fans, she called him, referring to the thick lashes protecting his expressive eyes. Walking toward him, she saw, as if they were palpable, Daniel's combination of strength and gentleness, the energy within him and the mellowness. His complexity made her want to spend her life figuring out this man.

Although Indianapolis was large enough for them to maintain anonymity, people still stared unabashedly when they walked arm in arm along the sidewalk. More than once someone, usually a man, sneered "whore" in passing. She didn't care, but Daniel could barely stand it that the woman he loved should be humiliated that way.

It was hard to believe no one had noticed a change in her. She felt so—so new. All those sentimental love songs didn't sound so mawkish anymore. In fact, at home or at work she went through every day humming a romantic tune, even dancing to it if she was alone. Couldn't everyone see *happiness* written all over her face? Surely discussions with friends revealed a more profound understanding of love, of men—of everything.

Before knowing him, she'd believed she could get along without the love of a man. Now she knew the intensity of emotion, the physical longing, the pain of separation. His tenderness touched her at a part of herself she'd never known existed. In other men she had detected sensitivity born of weakness, authority born of fear. Here was a man who had so much strength within that he could be gentle. She now knew how the heart and love had come to be connected in thought, for it was somewhere around her heart that she felt the painful joy. Or was it joyful pain?

Daniel marveled that any woman could understand him so thoroughly. Anna was able to reach into the dark recesses of his being and caress the hurts. Some he had developed scar tissue over; others were so sensitive he had spent years covering them with layer upon layer of protective gauze. She had touched them all.

She had touched them with her softness. Funny, he thought, independent, self-assured women seldom seemed soft. She was though. Not like vaporous cotton candy, sweet and quickly consumed, but like a quality cotton ball, moving across his being without heaviness, holding firmly together through compress and release.

Daniel: "There was something about Anna that made me feel I could share with her more than I had ever shared with anyone before. I felt acceptance and support. I felt free to admit certain things to her, such as weaknesses, feelings. I took a step I had never before taken: I let her into my interior. Something about her made me think, here's a person I can trust. Besides, she was a very intelligent and discerning woman. I think I felt I could open up to her, and she would be able to understand things no one else had ever been able to understand. Other people thought I was just a hard-headed, stubborn individual. She accepted me and understood in a different way."

Self-reliant, accustomed to doing things themselves, making their own decisions—by having these qualities in common, they each recognized in the other the loneliness that can accompany autonomy. They discerned in the other a beautiful vulnerability masked by a self-sufficient exterior born of survival instincts.

IT WAS TIME to tell family and a few friends about Daniel. But how? To say, *I'm in love with a Negro*, immediately made race the primary issue. But Anna didn't want acquaintances to be startled upon first seeing him.

She'd start with Inez, her closest college friend, who was working in Elgin, just west of Chicago. "Let's meet at the International House at the University of Chicago," Anna wrote from northern Indiana. "By the way, I'm bringing a friend with me, a man. I must tell you, he's colored."

Decades later Inez recalled that meeting clearly. After they'd been introduced, Daniel invited her to join Anna and him for dinner. At the time it didn't occur to Inez that he wasn't allowed to eat in most white-owned restaurants; in hindsight she saw the additional problem of his escorting two young white women.

He took them to a black restaurant. For Inez, it was a cultural shock. In her eighties she chuckled thinking that Daniel surely noticed how she was trying to get her bearings. The restaurant was filled with upscale, sophisticated black patrons, and the background music was black music, lively with a heavy beat. It was a pleasant meal, filled with animated, interesting conversation, and she was struck by how attractive Daniel was, how urbane he seemed.

Anna and Daniel didn't bring up the topic of their relationship, and Inez wasn't about to be unduly inquisitive, though she couldn't help but notice the affectionate gazes they exchanged. On the train back to Elgin her head was full with questions.

Later Anna wrote to say that she and Daniel were getting married. Inez replied with a frank letter in which she warned her friend of the problems a racist society would inflict on the couple and their children. Anna kept Inez's letters, this one among them:

"As you know my first impression of Daniel was pleasant. I could easily see how you are attracted to him. I saw intelligence, open-mindedness, idealism, and a strong sense of individualism. There was also a touch of the romantic and the adventurer. I liked Daniel. I'll continue to like him as long as he makes you radiantly happy."

The positive declaration was, however, followed by words of caution: "You must be prepared for the onslaught which will sweep over you if you ignore the customs of society, wrong though they be."

In a subsequent letter Inez wrote, "I knew when I saw you with him that here was something you'd never had. But please, Anna, pay attention to your head as well as to your heart.... Something in your makeup relishes playing a game in which the odds are against you. Risk is not a danger signal but a 'go' signal for you. Understanding yourself as a risk-taker demands that you learn to exercise some controls over your life.

"I want you to be sure that you know yourself, Anna. Here's where I'm going to be a bit tough. You have, as part of your inheritance, a trait of unpredictability, a willingness to invite the unusual and the unknown. Remember, if by marrying Daniel you are trying to set into motion a new stream of humanity, utmost strength will be required of you."

Except for Inez, nearly all of Anna's friends were social workers, women trained to suspend judgment and empathize. When she told them her news, they didn't show shock. Instead nearly everyone expressed apprehension about her future: how the communities in which she and Daniel would live would treat them, who their circle of acquaintances would be. But as each conversation began to wind down, friends never failed to mention how Anna glowed when she talked of Daniel.

Anna: "I knew my friends had my best interests at heart. No one came right out and said, 'Don't do this.' People who knew me knew the marriage would take place, and they accepted it. But they were worried about how the wider society would accept us. Some friends expressed concern about the children that would result from our marriage. That idea was and still is an absurdity. It's as though the biracial couple is creating the problem, when society is actually responsible for it.

"In growing up I'd been given a lot of independence, and I was accustomed to making my own decisions. I had pretty much relied on myself since I was twelve. Living with a sister isn't like living with a father and mother. So if I wanted to marry this man, I, not anyone else, would determine whether our marriage was in my best interests. I guess I was kind of like Daniel. If there was something I wanted to do, I assumed I would be able to handle whatever came along."

A TEA TOWEL in hand, wearing cotton stockings and a floral apron over her cotton housedress and long brown wool sweater, Violet met Anna at the door with exclamations of surprise and delight.

"What brings you to Richmond?" Before Anna could answer, while she was still untying her scarf and taking in the familiarity of the living room—with its mahogany Chippendale secretary, dark green sofa and chair, and stacks of *Readers Digest* on the coffee table—Violet, as was her habit, was thinking aloud, not pausing between thoughts. "I'll go fix us some Nescafe, George's working tonight, he'll want to see you too, the girls just went to bed, go say hello."

Which took longer than mother or aunt would have expected. In flannel pajamas, demonstrating a loquacity characteristic of healthy, happy six- and nine-year-olds, Myra and Joyce went through their individual litanies of the day's events while Anna laughed lustily. After kissing both on the forehead, she went out, softly closing the door behind her.

The war, which necessitated the rationing of home heating oil, was forcing Americans to tolerate colder homes. Returning to the living room, Anna appreciated Violet's efforts to combat winter's chill: the drawn ivy-patterned living room draperies, two steaming cups of Nescafe on the coffee table. Anna took a seat at the end of the sofa nearest the overstuffed chair where Violet sat in her harried-mother pose: arms flung over the sides of the chair, legs extended straight in front of her. In the background the radio quietly played the big-band sound of Glenn Miller, whose plane had gone down a few weeks earlier over the English Channel.

Anna took a sip of the bitter brew. With the end of coffee rationing, but the consumption of sugar still limited, many Americans were drinking their coffee black or with a little milk. She, on the other hand, used her twelve ounces a week to sweeten coffee. Violet baked cookies and let the girls sweeten their cereal.

In preparation for this visit, Anna had reminded herself that she was coming not to seek approval but to inform, though approval certainly would be the preferred response. She'd carefully developed a strategy that would approach the subject of the imminent wedding in a composed, rational way. However, now that she sat in Violet's living room, she suddenly lacked confidence that this conversation would go the way she intended. Her strategy might establish the initial tone, but Violet's response was unpredictable. There was a good chance that once she said *I'm going to marry this man,* the nature of the sisters' relationship would change. Permanently.

Almost as though Violet were speaking in a distant room, her voice echoing off the walls, Anna heard one the girls was "...getting A's in school... The teacher... commented..." Eyes downcast, Anna cradled the cup of Nescafe in both hands, drawing warmth from it. Confidence too.

Even when Anna had still lived in Richmond, Violet, who knew her better than anyone, did not notice the changes taking place, the alternating dreaminess and new enthusiasm for life. In all the time Anna had known Daniel, her sister had never asked the pertinent questions: *Are you seeing someone? What's causing you to look so happy?*

"When I saw the look on Myra's face..."

Anna placed the cup and saucer on the coffee table. "Violet," she interrupted, "I came this evening to tell you about something very important."

Violet abruptly stopped speaking. Lowering her chin to her chest so she could peer over the top of her wire-rimmed glasses, she asked, "What is it?"

"I'm in love. I'm going to be married in two weeks."

There, she'd said it, more quickly and bluntly than intended, but the words were out there.

Violet blinked her eyes and shook her head as if to clear her brain of cobwebs. "Uh, uh, that's wonderful—I think it's wonderful. But two weeks? Does that mean...is this relationship...have you only known this man a short time?"

"No, I've known him for a few years. I've thought everything through carefully."

"Is he from up in northern Indiana?"

"No, he's from Richmond."

Violet's eyebrows came together in puzzlement. She was biting her upper lip, probably wondering how something this important had slipped past her, wondering too that as close as they were, why Anna hadn't told her sooner.

"Is it anyone I know?"

"No. His name's Daniel Winters. Violet, the reason I haven't told you before now is because—because there's—Daniel is a Negro."

Anna leaned forward, elbows on her thighs, hands clasped in front of her. She said nothing more. Violet, instead of meeting Anna's gaze, looked down and watched her shoe push a small ball of fuzz across a patch of rug.

"How did you meet him?" she finally asked.

"When I was working for the Unemployment Relief office. We worked in the same building."

"Wellll...I guess...you...you'll have to bring this Daniel over so we can meet him....Uh...uh...why don't...why don't you bring…why don't you bring him over for pumpkin pie tomorrow night?"

THE TEMPERATURE HAD lingered in the low twenties all day. As they walked up the sidewalk to Violet's and George's little white house on A Street, Daniel's arm drawing her body close to his, he hummed, "I've got my love to keep me warm."

Violet would probably manage to be civil, a cool civility perhaps, and whereas George lacked many social graces, he could be depended on not to create a scene.

Daniel didn't know what to expect. As religious people, his future brother- and sister-in-law might demonstrate the same open, accepting qualities Anna had. Yet his experience had taught him never to assume white people would be friendly.

Was it the couple's own uneasiness about the evening, or did it, in fact, take a long time for Violet to answer their knock? Then seeing her in the doorway—the tightness of her brow, the firmness of the lines around her mouth—Anna recognized her sister's determined expression. But determined to be or do what? Not let her disapproval ruin the evening? Or was she determined to prevent this marriage?

Walking through the living room, past the comfortable sofa and easy chair, Violet led them into the small room off the kitchen. Three chairs to the dining room table formed a triangle. Without speaking, Violet motioned them to sit.

"I'll go say hello to the girls," Anna said.

"They're already in bed."

"I'll just stick my head in the door. They're not asleep yet, are they?"

"I'd rather you not disturb them." Ah, so she wanted to keep aunt and nieces separated. To make sure the girls didn't meet Daniel?

The three sat in awkward silence before Daniel said, "This is a lovely home you have. How long have you lived here?"

"Almost three years." She was quiet a moment. "George won't be able to join us. He has a sick headache."

"I'm sorry to hear that," Daniel said. "I understand they can be dreadful."

"Yes, he feels pretty bad."

"Well, at least you can get a little acquainted with Daniel tonight," Anna said, forcing a light-hearted tone. "There'll be plenty of future opportunities for the four of us to be together." Her smile evoked no similar pleasantry from Violet. Instead, pursed lips made it clear Violet did not want to deal with the possibility that this alliance would be permanent.

For almost an hour Daniel and Anna tried to make friendly conversation while Violet responded with cool politeness. No mention was made of pumpkin pie. There was no sign of George.

Leaving the house Anna half wished she'd gone ahead and married Daniel, then told Violet and George.

As Joyce later recalled, "Mom nearly had a nervous breakdown over it."

DANIEL: "MY COLORED friends were mixed in their reactions. I told my mother we were going to get married. Otherwise I didn't keep it a secret, but I didn't go out and broadcast it either. There were several problems with staying in Richmond. I grew up there, and my first wife lived there. We had had close friends together. None of them were disrespectful or antagonistic toward Anna, but it's hard for friends to figure out how to relate to the new situation. They're puzzled about what to do. I was used to associating with this group, but now there was a drastic change in my life that caused me to forsake all my other relationships."

ACCORDING TO KATHLEEN BLEE, in *Women of the Klan,* "The Klan reserved its greatest terror for nonwhite men who were 'involved with' white women."[18] In 1923, in Franklin, Indiana, the Klan burned crosses in celebration of a successful recruitment campaign. The crowd of 3000 cheered when a speaker "swore that with the Klan's ascendancy to power, Anglo-Saxon and Negro blood would never again mix."[19]

Although by the 1940s the revived Klan of the twenties had already burned itself out, the movement, nonetheless, had become embedded in the family, inspiring mothers to teach its values to their children. Many white Hoosiers still held firmly to the belief that mixing the blood, i.e. marriage between races, went against God's law.

BROOM, DUSTPAN, BOXES stacked atop boxes forced the driver to rely on the outside mirrors for visibility. Daniel had stored some of his belongings with his mother, and one of Anna's friends was going to ship a trunk, but basically, they were relying on the contents of the car for setting up housekeeping.

Because Indiana law prohibited marriage "between a white person and a person of one-eighth or more Negro blood," they were headed for Chicago, where they had an appointment to get married. From Chicago they planned to drive on to Minneapolis, more than 650 miles from an ex-wife, disapproving sister, and biased acquaintances. Besides having a reputation for being an open-minded city, Minneapolis also had a Harvester plant. A transfer had come through for Daniel.

Gas was still being rationed during most of 1945, so how the newlyweds managed to drive to Minneapolis by way of Chicago isn't clear. Perhaps because Daniel worked in the defense industry he could get a green B sticker, which allowed the car owner to purchase eight gallons a week. Or maybe, if a company had military contracts, allowance was made to transfer from one plant to another. In any case, Daniel and Anna would have been careful not to go out of their way for any superficial reason and would have stuck to the national speed limit of thirty-five miles per hour. To go faster was viewed as disloyal to the war effort.

What began as lethargic flurries just as they passed Richmond's city limits became almost blizzard conditions by the time they reached Gary. Yet snow seemed a happy portent, for it had fallen the night Anna first attended Daniel's class. Deciding "Winter Wonderland" should be *their* song, they crooned, "He'll say, 'Are you married?' We'll say, 'Yes, man.' We did it in Chicago, Illinois," until the thick white curtain forced them to keep their eyes on the road rather than exchange romantic glances.

They planned to stop in Gary and briefly visit Mattie, a Negro woman with whom Anna had developed a friendship when she worked in the Gary office. But by the time they arrived, driving conditions had become so wretched they decided to spend the night at Mattie's and catch the train into Chicago the next day.

The Chicago taxi driver who took them from the train station to the church was not in the most pleasant of moods. Hampered by the weather, he complained about street conditions, other drivers, pedestrians—everything and everybody that could be construed to be accountable for the disruptions to the flow of traffic. Snuggled together in the back seat the lovers could not share his frustrations. They had made an appointment to marry at eleven-thirty and allowed plenty of time to get to the church.

Dressed in a street-length dusty-rose velvet dress with a matching veiled hat, Anna vowed before a Reverend Mumford and his wife that, forsaking all others, she would love Daniel for better or for worse, for richer or poorer, in sickness and health, until they were separated by death. He made the same pledge.

Among her mementos, Anna still had the white folder embossed with pink flowers that contained a copy of their wedding ceremony and the marriage license dated February 2, 1945.

THE ADVICE, *STICK to your own kind,* has been around a long time. If you're Protestant, don't marry a Catholic; if you're a Jew, don't marry a Christian; if you're from a wealthy family, don't marry someone who's poor. However, in only one category did state legislators deem it necessary to enact a law limiting choice in marriage: the category of race.[20]

In what is now the U.S. the first law preventing marriage between races was established in 1664 by the Maryland colony, which was concerned about the number of white servant women marrying slave men. Would their offspring be slave or free? Other colonies followed suit in establishing laws against miscegenation (marriage between people of different races).

After the Civil War white men of the South became obsessed with the idea that black men wanted white women. Again, it was a matter of property, except now women were the possession. A white father whose daughter ran off with a black man couldn't control his property. If a white man's wife had a child by a black man, the white man couldn't control his property. There was a further complication: A woman was to be subservient to her husband, but a black person was to be subservient to a white person. So in a marriage between a white woman and a black man, who would be subservient to whom?[21] Why, the whole social order would be upset.

Over time thirty-three states banned some form of interracial marriage.[22] Such laws, however, failed to keep black women and white men, black men and white women apart, a fact demonstrated by the genealogy of the Delany sisters.[23] Their great-great grandmother was white and the wife of an army officer. While he was off fighting the War of 1812, she had two daughters by a slave. When the husband returned from the war, he was magnanimous and adopted the mixed-race girls as his own, which meant they were free but considered Negro. One of them, the Delany sisters' great grandmother, had four daughters by white men—perhaps by the same one, the sisters did not know. Still, though the four daughters were only one quarter black and born free rather than slave, they were considered Negroes. This created a marriage dilemma: they could not legally marry a white man, but nearly all black men were slaves. The Delany sisters' grandmother spent her adult life married in spirit, though not in the law, to a white man.

In 1949, four years after Anna and Daniel married, Indiana was one of eleven states in which miscegenation was a felony. It was a misdemeanor in five states. "According to Indiana Code 44-104 (which was in effect in 1945) such marriages were declared void. The penalty...included fines of 'not less than one hundred dollars or more than one thousand dollars, and imprisonment in a state prison not less than one year or more than ten years.'"[24] When antimiscegenation laws were challenged, state courts continued to uphold them on one of the following grounds: making laws about marriage is a prerogative of the state; natural law dictates that the races not intermarry; non-whites are physically and mentally inferior; or marriage between people of different races threatens the order and peace of the community.[25]

Not until 1967, in Loving v. Virginia, did the U.S. Supreme Court declare antimiscegenation laws unconstitutional. The case involved the marriage, in 1958, of a black woman and a white man from Virginia who married in Washington D.C., where there were no laws prohibiting marriage between races. When they returned to Virginia to live, they were indicted for breaking the law and sentenced to a year in jail. Instead of forcing them to serve the sentence, the judge instructed them to leave Virginia and not return for twenty-five years. These were the judge's words: "Almighty God created races white, black, yellow, malay, and red, and he placed them on separate continents....[B]ut for the interference with this arrangement there would be no cause for such marriages. The fact that he separated the races shows that he did not intend for the races to mix."[26] The Supreme Court, however, ruled that "the freedom to marry, or not marry, a person of another race resides within the individual and cannot be infringed by the State."[27]

Recent years have brought a dramatic change in American attitudes toward interracial marriage. In 2011 the Pew Research Center reported that 14.6 percent, or one in seven, of all new marriages were between persons of different races or ethnicities. "In 1961, the year Barack Obama's parents were married, less than one in 1,000 new marriages in the United States was, like theirs, the pairing of a black person and a white person, according to Pew Research estimates. By 1980, that share had risen to about one in 150 new marriages. By 2008, it had risen to one-in-sixty."[28]

UNTIL 1945, FOUR years into the war, Daniel had avoided the draft, which first took eighteen to twenty-five year olds, then husbands with one child, then those with two children. When men with three children were called, five months prior to his marrying Anna and moving to Minneapolis, Daniel received his notification to report for duty. At that time he was working on gear hobs at the Richmond plant.

"Daniel, I understand you received your greetings," one of the assistant superintendents yelled over the noise of the machine the following day.

"Yes, I did."

"You're too valuable. I can't let you go."

Two days later Daniel learned that because he was on defense work he would be exempt for six more months—information that apparently didn't get forwarded to the Minneapolis plant. His first day on the new job, with only one month left on his deferment, he was filling out various forms in the personnel office. With the plant strictly on war contract, everywhere he turned people in military uniform were milling around.

Standing before a young white woman studying his papers, he watched her brightly painted nails move across the lines of print then come to rest halfway down the page. Rhythmically her index finger tapped the counter, paused a moment, then resumed its beat. Without looking up, she said, "I see you're a college graduate."

"Yes."

"You know Spanish and German."

"I know Spanish, just a little German."

She lifted her eyes to accusingly meet his. "You don't have any business being exempt. You should be in the Signal Corps."

Oh, boy, he thought, *I just got married, moved my wife up here, and now I'm going to be drafted.*

The woman dismissed him, requesting that he wait in a large reception area through which scores of khaki-clad people passed—as though to remind him of his lack of patriotism.

"Mr. Winters, I'm Harold van Ness." A tall man near retirement age interrupted his thoughts. "About this matter of your military duty, I think we can get you exempted for another six months."

That was February. The war ended in August.

Daniel: "But I wouldn't have gone. I would have gone to jail first. I didn't have any freedom to defend on some European beach or Pacific island. Most Negroes felt the same, but they acquiesced and went to war anyway. In the United States colored men were hardly considered men at all. White folks, fearing what we might do with knowledge, had sent us to separate schools, inferior schools. The doors of higher education, the professions, political power, had been barricaded. In much of the country, tired from hard physical work, we had been forced to stand on crowded buses while white men and women sat. It was their, white folks', liberty I would have been jeopardizing my life for, not mine. My job in Minneapolis freed me from the draft long enough to keep me out of jail."

THEY SAT ON the living room sofa holding each other in grief as they listened to the radio. They knew the president suffered from the vestiges of polio. But dead! And so suddenly! "I have a terrific headache," Morgan Bailey reported Roosevelt saying. Correspondents in the press room were crying. The cabinet was meeting at that very minute. Truman was about to be sworn in. Whether people admired or hated FDR, the whole nation was in shock.

In the weeks that followed, Daniel and Anna spent every evening beside the radio, absorbing as much news as possible of rapidly changing world events. At the end of April Mussolini was captured and executed; Hitler committed suicide. May 8 was declared V-E Day, Victory in Europe. The war that had dominated the lives of Americans from the beginning of Daniel's and Anna's courtship was over in Europe and appeared to be approaching its end in Asia.

Buchenwald, Auschwitz, Dachau. Foreign words became part of their vocabularies, gruesome topics for dinner conversation. For Daniel and Anna, as for many Americans who read newspapers, magazines such as *Time,* and listened to the news on the radio, the horrors that had transpired in these places were nearly impossible to fathom. As were the atomic bombs the U.S. dropped on Nagasaki and Hiroshima, Japan. The war wrecked unprecedented devastation, with about 60 million people dying from combat, bombings, disease, and starvation. German and Japanese cities had been leveled; Great Britain had suffered extensive bombing. Over one million Americans died.

In the final days of the war Anna found a job as a social worker, and they bought a duplex in a mixed neighborhood. Minneapolis was a friendly town for a biracial couple. Cultural events, friends, and—as soon as weather permitted—tennis convinced them that the new life they were building together was going to be of the happily-ever-after variety.

Minneapolis might have been their permanent home had Daniel's mother not again taken ill in 1947. They made the difficult decision to return to Richmond to live with her. Anna was now a guest in Daniel's mother's home, and while Pearl was too weak to be the forceful woman she'd always been, she remained the one around whom the house was organized. Her presence required attentiveness and allowed the couple few private moments.

The move also affected their social life. While in Minneapolis they'd been able to form friendships with black, white, and mixed couples; in Richmond opportunities for friendship were limited. Neighbors, most of them black, didn't seem to be bothered by the marriage, but they took no initiative toward the couple, and there were no social ties to the white community. Although Daniel later made white friends through the labor union and invited a few into their home, the invitations were seldom reciprocated.

His cousin and her husband, one of the few couples Daniel and Anna were close to, introduced them to the Interstate Bridge Club, a group of black couples. But everyone in the club, including Daniel's cousin, was considerably older, many with children Daniel had known when growing up.

With the Bridge Club their only opportunity for social interaction, Daniel and Anna spent most of their free time alone. Yet they were limited in the things they could do outside of home. Restaurants would not serve them, and when they went to a movie, they sat in the balcony reserved for Negroes. They danced at home. Prevented from participating in the life of the community, they created a world inhabited by only the two of them. At work Daniel would reach into his pants pocket and find a piece of paper: "I love you, Big Lug." Under his pillow he would discover a note saying "It was snowing," referring to the night Anna went to observe him teach his class. He wrote poems about their love and crooned "My Heavenly Dream," a song he'd composed for her during their courtship.

Though their marriage was illegal in Indiana, there were no efforts to prosecute them. Why? "If they were citizens of 'this state' (Indiana) than it appears they could have been charged. The failure to arrest them may indicate county prosecutorial discretion rather than the state's unwillingness to enforce."[29]

In the three years they had been away, Anna had tried to maintain a correspondence with Violet and George. Violet had written sporadically, but her letters seemed distant, and she never mentioned Daniel's name. Let them take the initiative, Anna decided upon their return to Richmond.

How Violet could love her but not Daniel sometimes occupied Anna's thoughts. Here was her closest relative, who'd had a heart big enough to welcome her little sister to live in her home but now could not be hospitable to the man she loved. Wasn't expansiveness central to the concept of family? A family was supposed to reach out and draw new people in: new children, new spouses, sometimes even a total stranger.

More than two months passed before Violet called, feebly attempted light conversation, and issued an invitation for Sunday dinner. But the invitation was only to Anna, who replied that she wouldn't go without Daniel. Acting as though misunderstood, Violet said, no, she meant they were both to come.

Seated at the table that Sunday, Anna had the feeling Violet's primary fear was for her children, that she wanted to shelter them—from what? The girls, however, seemed oblivious to the tension among the grown-ups. Myra wasn't satisfied unless she could sit beside Daniel at the table, and after the meal Joyce clearly appreciated the attention he gave her artwork.

In the ensuing years the girls showed no hesitancy about accepting him. Myra proudly introduced him to friends as *Uncle Daniel,* and in her teen years Joyce often sought his advice. Unable to talk with either of her parents as honestly as she could with Daniel, she brought him confidences that revealed her delight and fears about relating to boys. Violet and George, though, continued to treat Daniel with coolness. In fairness, though, as members of the Church of the Brethren they may have disapproved of his divorce and remarriage. Or maybe race really was the primary issue. In either case they seemed convinced that the one whom they had practically raised as their own daughter had chosen to marry the *wrong* man.

Chapter 8

*A*S THEY DO *every morning, voices on the sidewalk beneath the bedroom window rouse Anna from sleep. People going to work. Women in pairs making their way to the market at the end of the block, their animated conversations carrying up to the second floor. She feels Daniel stirring beside her. She reaches over, tracing his brow with her finger. He opens one eye.*

She knows he's still ambivalent about the interview, telling this white woman, just because she's almost family, about his past. Six months ago, for more than a week they discussed whether to do this. Argued is more accurate.

"No use telling somebody about our lives if we can't be honest," he'd said, assuming they wouldn't tell the full story.

She won by promising they would speak of their relationship as if more recent events had never occurred. Besides, she urged, his life alone had the makings of a good story: fighting racial injustice, working hard to earn a college degree, eventually finding a job as a janitor. Later his success as a union officer.

She reaches over and turns on the radio. The dial is set on a station that broadcasts in English. Hidden in the morning news is an item that causes Daniel to bolt up in bed: Roy Cohn, chief counsel for Joseph McCarthy, has died. Of AIDS.

"Vindication!" Daniel exclaims.

IN 1941, WHILE still married to Martha, Daniel often paused outside the factory gates at the end of his shift to listen to Jack Carpenter, a union organizer from Chicago. Black metal lunch pails in hand, weary men congregated, a few, like Daniel, clustering around Carpenter. Most, though, lurked in the background lest management see them. The company's goal was to make as much money as it could, Carpenter said, and it didn't give a hoot about the workers. By uniting, organizing a union, the workers could unshackle themselves from the absolute control the company had over them.[30]

There was little doubt in the men's minds that Carpenter was right. Factory laborers had to work six days a week with no paid vacations, no paid holidays, and no benefits. Anyone unfortunate enough to get sick was quickly replaced by someone who was healthy. Conditions at the plant were hazardous, particularly in the foundry, where men worked with molten hot iron, and out on the tracks, where they did back-breaking tasks without the help of machinery. Workers were often severely burned or injured. Sometimes the company hired a new man, and a month later, without giving any reason, fired an employee who had been on the job five years. There was nowhere to go for redress. Before wartime production began, the fact that people still desperately needed jobs made them subject to the whims of business.

At first Daniel didn't approve of unions, but every day, when he got off work, exhausted and covered with grime, he couldn't help but think that a united work force was the only means to better conditions and better pay.

Daniel: "Here I was, a college graduate with little hope of using my skills or reaching my potential. As long as laborers were afraid to organize, they were powerless. Besides, if I joined the union, what did I have to lose?"

On a Sunday afternoon in late spring, four workers from Harvester met with Carpenter in the front parlor of Daniel's and Martha's home. Three weeks and four meetings later the smoke-filled room was packed, mostly with men but also with a few women. Sitting on kitchen chairs, footstools, and the floor, they strategized into the morning hours about organizing a local. In this setting a person's color wasn't as important as what he or she could contribute to the cause.

Martha, who had recently begun working at Harvester, served as a reluctant hostess. Fifteen cents an hour wasn't much, she said, but at least she had a job. In her mind Jack Carpenter could convince someone that grass was orange.

Daniel: "Martha often accused me of being a mal-content. 'What makes you think you're any better than any other colored person?' she'd ask. 'Do you think you shouldn't be limited by the color of your skin when all the rest of us are?' Not that she docilely accepted the limitations of race. She's an intelligent woman who stood her ground in many a racially tense situation."

The Richmond plant was the first International Harvester plant to organize. Aware that if one factory unionized others would follow, the company tried to frighten and isolate leaders.

Calling the strike in '41 was risky. The union was new and still unsure how much support it had among the workers. Its representatives spent hours at the negotiation table, trying to reach a contract with management, but couldn't get anywhere. Finally, on a Tuesday afternoon union leadership informed Harvester that a vote would be taken that night. A strike was inevitable.

Harvester immediately notified town officials, who had heard about strikes in other parts of the country, where picketing often went beyond disturbing the peace to people getting killed. Fearing the worst, the mayor called in state police. Town officials drove up to North Market Street, where they deputized every derelict, sober or drunk, they could find. For carrying out the duties of a deputy, each man was given five dollars and a heavy club.

For Daniel, as with all the others, this was his first time on a picket line. The mood outside the three-story brick building that first morning was solemn. No one knew what to expect. Though union leadership urged everyone not to resort to violence, strikers were prepared in case fighting broke out. They carried picket signs made of heavy oak and placed slices of rubber car tires under their hats.

They marched just outside the high chain-link fence chanting, "A fair day's wage for a fair day's work" and "In union there is strength." Police lined up the scabs—workers not participating in the strike—on the east side of Maple Street. At the sound of a police whistle, the scabs moved toward the plant entrance, filing through the gate and into the building. Though he joined other picketers in booing, Daniel felt torn. These were women and men he knew and in many cases respected. Some naively believed management's campaign against the union;

others were in such financial straits they thought they dare not take the risk.

No sooner were the scabs inside the plant, than chaos erupted. The deputized derelicts charged the strike line, swinging their clubs and yelling obscenities. Daniel heard one of them shout, "For years I've been put in jail for fighting. Today I'm getting paid for it."

In spite of union efforts to keep the strike peaceful, it turned out to be characterized by violence. The union blamed the police department; Harvester and the police blamed the union. But as a result workers got their first contract, and their pay went up to thirty cents an hour with paid holidays.

FOR UNIONS THE WAR posed a dilemma. It necessitated increased production, creating more jobs. With so many men fighting abroad, there were openings for women and African Americans, now protected from discrimination in defense industries. Unions welcomed both groups; membership swelled. This would have resulted in increased muscle had strong national support for the war not motivated both the AFL and CIO, umbrella groups for the specialized unions, to pledge not to strike during this time of national crisis.

Daniel: "The war enabled big companies to co-op the unions. The companies could help the cause of war and make a lot more money through increased production. They knew this could only be done by eliciting the cooperation of the workers. They used all the patriotic words. During this time I was on the Production Drive Committee. In those meetings you would have thought the company was a religious organization. They were concerned about the good of the nation, the good of the worker. They'd use accolades to get you to see their point of view, but once the meeting was adjourned their concerns disappeared."

Daniel's involvement in the union continued after he and Anna married and moved to Minneapolis. Indeed, his brief stay there (1945-47) may well have strengthened his commitment to labor, as Minneapolis, a transportation hub for goods delivered throughout the Midwest, was already a union town. Eleven years earlier a group of Trotskyites, under the leadership of Ferrell

Dobbs, had radicalized Minneapolis truckers. Their successful, though bloody, strike of 1934 contributed to labor being strengthened nationwide. It also played a key role in the passage of the Wagner Act (1935), a federal law that limited employers' interference with workers' rights to organize in collective bargaining through unions. During Daniel's and Anna's stay in Minneapolis, Hubert Humphrey, a friend of labor who would later run for the presidency of the United States, served as mayor.

After Daniel's return to Richmond in 1947, the local of the Farm Equipment Workers Union elected him publicity director time and again. (Later he would serve as president.) Articulate and educated, he carried responsibilities in public speaking and producing written communications. If a worker was fired, by the time his shift was over, Daniel was handing out flyers that told what had happened and what action the union planned to take. Before a strike he'd be on the radio trying to nurture public sympathy. This was a difficult task given Richmond's self-perception of being a peaceful, friendly town. Its citizens didn't like disruptions.

Though the union kept pushing for a decent living wage for members, grievances weren't always economic in nature. Concerns included policies about fair hiring and firing, sick leaves, and establishing a reasonable number of breaks during the workday. As long as International Harvester refused to hear grievances, the union went on strike, sometimes every year.

If violence broke out, the union was blamed. Just for talking loudly, picketers would be arrested and charged with disturbing the peace. That is, if they were men. Knowing the police would never put their hands on a woman, female strikers could be shockingly aggressive. Many taunted police, "Touch me, if you dare, you big fat ass son-of-a-bitch!" Officers would turn red in the face, but that was all.

By all appearances, the *Palladium-Item,* Richmond's newspaper, was in alliance with Harvester. During one strike the newspaper carried screaming headlines that Daniel's friend Carl, treasurer of the union, was being questioned for the bombing of a scab's house. Radios carried the story too. Carl was released because of inconclusive evidence, but the negative publicity about a union officer being a crime suspect damaged union credibility and his reputation. Later he put his wife on a train for an indefinite visit to relatives in Philadelphia.

Strikes were especially hard on union leaders' wives, who never knew when their husband might be arrested or come home beat up. Listening to the radio every evening, Anna dreaded learning that Daniel or someone she knew had gone to jail or been injured. For union leaders there was the additional fear that their families might be victims of reprisals.

DANIEL HAD SET the alarm for four o'clock. Half an hour later he was headed to the union office where he intended to mimeograph a flyer explaining the current strike to the citizens of Richmond. Anna had slept in until six-thirty and was getting ready for work when she heard an insistent knock at the front door. Gathering her chenille robe tighter for a more modest appearance, she walked with quick steps to answer it. Her thoughts raced to the possible harm that might have already come to Daniel that morning. Seeing a police officer didn't mollify her.

The officer filled the doorway with his large frame. "I came by to tell your husband to quit following my wife," he said.

"I beg your pardon?" The cold February air rushed in. Briefly she considered inviting the man into the living room, since he was already on the threshold anyway, then decided against it.

The officer thrust his chin to the side and lifted his shoulders as if trying to appear yet bigger. He repeated what he'd just said, this time more slowly and emphatically, as if she didn't understand the English language. "I came by to tell your husband to quit following my wife."

She knew how to use her own posture to advantage. Pulling her shoulders back and standing straight, she placed her hands on her hips and boldly looked up to meet his gaze. "What makes you think he's been following your wife?"

"He went out last night, didn't he?"

"Yes, for a short time." Daniel had driven over to Carl's house to drop off some papers related to union work, but been gone no more than ten minutes.

"My wife says he was following her in the car."

"That's preposterous."

"You calling my wife a liar?"As if he might at that moment use it, the officer placed a hand on the club at his side.

She ran her fingers through yet uncombed hair. "Even if someone did follow her, how would she have known it was Daniel?"

"She's seen his car parked in the driveway in front of this house."

Anna lifted her chin triumphantly. "Then maybe I'm the one who followed her."

"She knows it was him. You give your husband a message from me, you hear? Tell him I'm coming back sometime when he's home. And in the meantime, he'd better not follow my wife again. Tell him she's got a gun and I got a gun, you tell him that, you hear? And, like I said, you tell him I'll be back."

The moment the officer turned to leave, Anna quickly closed the door and locked it securely. So Daniel's concern for her safety hadn't been paranoia, after all. Though the man had come no further than the door, he had intruded in her home, into her life, his purpose, no doubt, to remind her that she too was vulnerable. Well, she had news for him: She would not be intimidated.

He never returned to the house.

DANIEL: "THE RICHMOND police were anything but *peace officers.* They joined civic leaders in a commitment to the status quo. They harassed union leaders, particularly those who were black. Often, I'd be waiting to cross a street, and an officer would step up alongside me, stick an elbow in my ribs or push me off the curb, and mutter 'hot-shot nigger' or 'smart-ass nigger.'"

Public support for the union was negligible. Residents whose families had lived in Richmond for many decades championed the causes of company managers, who belonged to the same clubs and lived in the same neighborhoods. Besides, if unions were strong in the big factories, what would prevent workers in the small piano or casket factories, which were locally owned, from organizing? To many of the town's leaders unions were a threat to a social order that had been around for more than a century.

Not only did the union run into opposition from those entrenched in the life and history of the community, but also from newly arrived white tenant farmers from the South. Hearing that a worker could make up to a hundred dollars a week, these people, many of them illiterate, had moved to Richmond. But they weren't able to secure the good jobs, and they had problems adjusting to urban life. They became resentful of blacks who had the jobs they wanted and of the unions, which offered security for those already employed.

In spite of Harvester's resolve and community ill will, each strike brought improved working conditions and resulted in strengthening the union. The union successfully pressured management to buy truck lifts, which increased safety for the men who worked out on the tracks, and it began to demand that women receive equal pay. Several years would pass before the company paid for insurance and hospitalization.

ANNA SAT WITH elbows on the kitchen table, chin cupped in her hands. She counted the strokes of the church clock two blocks away: six, seven, eight. In front of her a serving spoon stood at attention in a bowl of cold mashed potatoes; the peas were shriveled; the meatloaf on a platter looked dried out, unappetizing.

She heard the back door open, the screen door slam, the sound of Daniel's heavy work shoes entering, then a silence, which she knew meant he was removing them beside the door. His stocking feet thumped down the hallway in her direction. Instead of meeting him at the kitchen door and giving him her usual welcome-home kiss, she remained seated.

"I would have appreciated it if you had called to say you'd be late," she said.

"Well, one thing after another came up," he said curtly as he stepped over to the sink to wash his hands.

"But I was worried, the strike and all." She rose. Making two trips, she carried the food back to the stove for reheating, disappointed that what had taken more than an hour to prepare had no doubt lost its flavor. "Will you please call me the next time?" she said over her shoulder.

Massaging his forehead with his fingers, weariness imprinted on his brow, he dropped to the chair opposite the one she'd been sitting on.

"Quit sounding like a mother. If I say things came up, things came up. And I don't need you on my back."

She scraped the food into pans and wiped her hands on her floral-print apron. "I don't mean to be on your back. I'm just asking for some consideration, so I won't worry. A simple phone call."

"Anna," Daniel shouted, "I told you to get off my back. I will not have some woman leading me around by the nose."

Recognizing this was escalating into a non-discussion and not worth a major confrontation, Anna stepped away from the stove. She leaned on the edge of the table with both elbows and made a low guttural sound. "That's it, growl," she said playfully. "Growl at me, Daniel." As usual he laughed and the tension broke.

From the very beginning she'd recognized the anger he carried, an anger he explained and she understood as related to the racial prejudice he'd endured. He'd had to fight to accomplish the ordinary and to keep people from running over him.

Anna: "There were times when we were both intensely angry, but we worked things out. We worked them out because of the way we felt about one another. I remember once telling my cousin about our fights, and she was horrified. But back then making up was always wonderful. At that time I didn't take his anger personally; it was just the way he was. And no matter what the anger inducing incidents were, we were always able to come back together in love."

IN 1950 JOSEPH MCCARTHY of Wisconsin was elected to the United States Senate and quickly discovered the personal power that could be gained by arousing people's fears against communism. He would save this country by tracking down every communist who threatened the security of the nation. He targeted unions.

Daniel: "Without the union the worker stood alone, a powerless individual at the mercy of the company. The low pay and unsafe conditions made many American factories fertile soil for the labor movement and communism. The Communist Party put out a paper, *The Daily Worker*, which many union members subscribed to, not because it was a communist paper, but because it contained labor news. In those days there were a few communists in every one of them, but unions operated independently from the Communist Party. The issue they shared in common was a concern for workers.

"McCarthy was a company man, sympathetic to the big companies rather than to the workers. His way of breaking unions was to break their leadership. The Farm Equipment Union had communists in it—all the unions did—so McCarthy went after it. The pressure became so intense that those of us at International Harvester changed to the United Electrical Workers Union (UE), a much larger organization. We felt it was such a large union, McCarthy wouldn't dare attack it. But there were two UE men—a Lancaster and I don't remember the other man's name—who were personally attacked as being communists. That was when we really began to have problems over the issue."

Seated next to Carl on a hard wooden seat on the convention floor, having spent a long, long day listening to speech after speech, voting on measure after measure, Daniel was anxious to flee and take advantage of Chicago's nightlife. It wasn't often that he had the opportunity to escape the white world and completely immerse himself in a womb of Negro-ness and jazz.

"Ladies and gentlemen," a convention leader shouted, "Tonight we have a surprise for you. If you just remain in your seats a short time longer, you'll have a rare privilege, something to remember for a lifetime."

Daniel and Carl discussed whether they should stay or go ahead with their plans. There was plenty of night, they finally decided. They'd stay for the surprise, then take off for the South Side. Forty-five minutes went by. The audience grew restless, people standing to stretch, going outside for a smoke, heading for a restroom.

Then a commotion in the back of the auditorium drew everyone's attention, and a large black man flanked by body guards emerged. A piano was rolled out on the stage, a musician with it, and at the moment the large black man reached the piano's side, he began to sing.

The man was Paul Robeson, internationally known singer of opera, spirituals, and songs of the folk. As a young man he'd been an All-American football player at Rutgers University, valediction of his class, a graduate of Columbia Law School. It was on stage, however, as actor and singer (most notably for singing "Old Man River" in *Showboat*), that he came to prominence.

In 1924, at age twenty-six, Robeson had the leading male role in Eugene O'Neill's *All God's Chillun Got Wings*, a play about an interracial marriage. Mary Blair, a white actress, played the part of Robeson's wife, a woman who could not measure up to her husband in ambition or intellect. The play evoked public outcry. The Ku Klux Klan sent threatening letters to the actors and directors. (Almost a year prior to the production of O'Neill's play, in regard to another entertainment event, the Klan's paper, *The Fiery Cross,* had written, "The revolting spectacle of a white woman clinging to the arms of a colored man is simply beyond words to express."[31])

By the time Robeson sang before the UEWE convention, he was embroiled in another controversy: the U.S. government had branded him a communist. An activist in civil rights and labor movements throughout the world, he had expressed admiration for socialism and the Soviet Union, and when abroad he spoke openly and critically about the conditions of African Americans. Though the singer declared he had never been part of an international conspiracy and knew no one who had been, the government revoked his passport. For eight years, without a passport, he was denied the right to earn his living abroad. Never formally accused he, therefore, had no means of appeal.

The entertainment world expelled him, not even allowing him to use recording houses. Invited to sing the title song for the film, *Song of the Rivers*, Robeson had to record it in his brother's home. Shostakovich composed the score, Bertolt Brecht wrote the lyrics, and Picasso did the publicity poster, but the film was banned in the U.S.

The convention leader was right. It was an evening Daniel never forgot, partly because of the privilege of hearing the famous bass, but also because everyone in attendance was later pronounced guilty of being a communist. Guilty by association. It didn't matter that Robeson had once sung all over Europe, all over the world. That the government had labeled him a communist and that he sang before a union convention meant to a McCarthy-crazed country that those who heard him were communists.

Daniel considered Paul Robeson not a political activist but an artist who had a concern for social justice and world peace. Although Daniel's reputation was sullied by the event, the memory of the music and his pride in the talent of a Negro performer stayed with him. Identifying strongly with the singer's struggle, he collected Paul Robeson's records and read everything he could about his life.

Not long after returning home from the convention, Daniel and several other local union leaders were called to Indianapolis to be questioned by a subcommittee of the House Un-American Activities Committee. Similar hearings in Chicago probed the actions of higher level union officials. One by one local leaders were called in and directly asked, "Are you a communist?" When his turn came, Daniel said emphatically, no, he was not·a communist and had never been one.

But in the minds of many Richmond residents, Negroes, communists, and unions had become synonymous.

IT WAS PAST eleven at night. Along with another union leader, Daniel was working late in the union office, concentrating as he pecked away at the small typewriter with his index fingers.

When they heard the door handle turn, both men looked up to see two strangers in suits. Daniel, who always made an immediate assessment based on appearance, noticed that the shorter of the two men was neatly attired, his hair slicked down. The second man, wearing wrinkled pants, had a slouched posture and disheveled hair.

"We're looking for Daniel Winters," the slovenly dressed man said.

"I'm Daniel Winters."

The other man spoke: "We'd like to talk with you."

In a polite, respectful manner Daniel motioned toward two chairs. "Have a seat."

The shorter man said, "No, we'd rather you come out to the car with us. Something private."

Uncomfortable with this suggestion, Daniel considered refusing. Neither man looked like a thug. Much taller than either of them, he took a little comfort in his earlier training as a boxer. Besides, if he didn't return, the other union officer would call the police—though they certainly couldn't be depended on to come to his rescue. Yet there was something about these two men, the confidence with which they carried themselves, their assumption that he would do as they said. It quickly became apparent that he really didn't have a choice.

With a man on each side of him, he left the office and walked partway down the block to a parked '41 Ford sedan. The man in the wrinkled pants opened the back door and motioned Daniel in, then got in the passenger side of the front seat. The other man was already behind the steering wheel. As though choreographed, they turned around and flashed their FBI credentials in Daniel's face.

The well-groomed man held up a file, at least an inch thick, filled with onionskin papers. "We know quite a bit about you, Winters." He paused as though to make a greater impact. "You were born April 17, 1908. Your step-father, Clifford Thurman, died in 1921."

"Your mother later married Finley Level," his partner said, his words clipped. "You've worked as a brick mason, custodian, and hod carrier."

"You're married to Anna Harley, a white woman."

The night visitors were quiet for a moment as though they wanted the thoroughness of their knowledge to sink in.

"Do you take *The Daily Worker?*" the well-groomed man asked.

"If you know so much about me, you know I don't subscribe to *The Daily Worker.* But I do read it."

"Where do you get all the ideas for the union propaganda you put out?"

"They come from my head—and from my experience."

"Come on, your ideas come from *The Daily Worker,* don't they?"

"No. Everything I write, every speech I make—the ideas are all mine."

Whatever their purpose, these two worked fast. The neatly attired man closed the file, put it on the seat beside him, and turned back around to face the steering wheel. He turned the key in the ignition while the one with wrinkled pants got out and as he opened the back door, motioned for Daniel to leave.

Clenching his teeth, Daniel walked back to the office. Being questioned by the FBI at this time of night had served its likely purpose: he felt intimidated and frightened. Especially for Anna. Should he tell her about this evening? He didn't want her to live in fear, but he didn't want her to be caught off guard either. He decided not to tell her.

THE FBI AND local police were seldom subtle in reminding union leaders that their every move was being watched. When Daniel headed for work in the morning, when he came home in the evening, when he went out at night, there was always someone behind him. An agreement seemed to exist between the FBI and the local police. He came to assume that every officer in Richmond knew he worked at Harvester and the hours he was there.

In 1952, approximately thirty thousand Harvester workers in eight plants went out on strike. The strike came during the heat of McCarthyism and was particularly bitter because of the mood of the country. The company, confident that public sentiment would now go even more strongly against the union, was particularly difficult to negotiate with. It shrewdly maneuvered to cut wages and end the contract, all the time using the press to proclaim that the union was being unreasonable.

The 1952 strike lasted twelve weeks. As it dragged on, men who found it particularly hard to keep food on the table would go back into the shop for a short time to earn some cash. The restaurant across the street from the factory served as a soup kitchen, where a worker's family could eat. Day after day during that period Daniel would awaken at two or three o'clock in the morning, go to the union office, then be on the picket line at six. Given the volatility of people's emotions, control was more likely if a union official was on hand at all times. Evenings he worked late at the office, preparing for radio interviews and writing publicity materials.

Public relations professionals told the company's side in attractive glossy booklets, full-page ads in the paper, and half-hour radio programs. Their message: the company was losing money and couldn't afford to give workers a raise.

By comparison the union's efforts seemed amateur. Every week Daniel gave a five-minute radio talk called "Strike News and Labor Views." A used machine cranked out mimeographed letters and flyers, and small paid ads in the paper explained the worker's side. In all of this the press was anything but neutral. The company's version was often printed as factual news, while the union's version only became known through ads. The union told reporters it was ready to resume negotiations as soon as the old contract was reinstated without wage cuts. The paper printed a long list of nonexistent union demands and sympathetically stated that the company refused to negotiate on so many demands at once. Wanting the public to see for itself what was going on, union leaders challenged International Harvester to put the negotiations on TV, but the company refused.

The city court's bail for arrested strikers was excessive, according to a newspaper article about a state Superior Court judge's ruling. But an adjoining column reported that on the previous day the FBI had arrested three *small fry* communist party leaders from three states on charges of "conspiring to advocate the overthrow of the United States government." One of the persons was described as "an official of the United Electrical Workers of America...(a) union (that) has been expelled from the CIO on grounds of communist domination." Anyone reading the newspaper might be led to believe that the local union, the Farm Equipment division of the United Electrical Workers Union (FE-UE), was a communist organization.

Melvin Jordan, an international representative of the FE-UE and a consultant to the Richmond local, was arrested for allegedly assaulting scabs. Local union leaders were convinced he'd been arrested so the company could get his name before the public. Sure enough, four days after Jordan's arrest, a newspaper article revealed that a witness before a congressional subcommittee on education identified *the wife of Jordan's attorney* as a member of the Communist Party. The article also said that Jordan was to have appeared before the committee but refused to answer questions without the presence of his attorney, a sure sign of guilt.

On another day a newspaper article about the strike appeared next to a column about the central library in Indianapolis removing an adult education book, *English for Workers,* from the shelves because it contained "chapter after chapter of pro-communist propaganda."

To be questioned about membership in the Communist Party, union leaders discovered, was to have their position at the bargaining table weakened. Although local leadership was neither directly accused nor convicted of having communist ties, in the eyes of the community these men were guilty.

Anna: "During those days when Daniel was involved in the union, I was working for the Indiana State Department. The people in the children's division formed a union, which, after I quit working for the state, was maligned as being filled with communists. Two of my friends, Clara and Maggie, were active in the Union of Child Workers, and they were accused of being communists. The times being as they were, the whole organization was tainted by accusations that didn't have to be substantiated. Clara and Maggie found that old friends wouldn't even speak to them anymore, for fear of being labeled themselves.

"I had some other good friends who had always stopped to see me on their frequent trips through Richmond. Suddenly they no longer came to visit. It was very peculiar. The Indianapolis paper often carried articles that mentioned Daniel's name and his union involvement. So I finally figured these old friends didn't want to risk tarnishing their name by visiting with me. It reached the point where people were afraid to talk to their neighbors for fear they might be spies. Maybe the family next door was reporting something to the FBI or local police. No one could trust anyone else."

Daniel: "I didn't agree with everything that unions did. But they sometimes had to take questionable actions to protect the workers, because the workers didn't have anyone else to protect them. Workers would never have got increases in wages; working conditions and safety conditions would never have improved if it hadn't been for the pressure of unions. I am anti-communist, but I'm thankful to them in respect to unions. If it hadn't been for the communists, the labor movement would never have been started."

In 1957 International Harvester closed its Richmond plant. If workers were willing to relocate they could have jobs at other plants. Daniel and Anna decided not to move, but no one else in town would hire Daniel. In their eyes he was a communist troublemaker.

THERE WERE AMONG Daniel's collection of memorabilia, tucked away in file cabinet drawers and boxes, several items pertaining to his union days. A page from a company magazine called "Our employees and their families" highlights the jobs of black workers. There is a picture of Daniel, dressed in a recently laundered white shirt and bib overalls, shoveling the shavings; another of a *janitress*, a flower in her hair, wiping a countertop in the dispensary; and a picture of Daniel's friend Carl loading a truck of sheet steel. *We care about our colored employees*, the pictures seem to convey.

A booklet released by International Harvester explains the 1952 strike from the company's point of view. In the booklet the company states: "During all the years Harvester has dealt with FE-UE [Farm Equipment-United Electrical], the character of the union leadership has never changed. It was and is the company's belief that the principle leaders of the union were either themselves communists, or were communist sympathizers and fellow-travelers."

On onion skin paper is a carbon copy of Daniel's statement to a hearing of the House Committee on Agriculture and Forestry, October 19,1953, at Indianapolis, Indiana.

Statement presented by District Nine, United Electrical,
Radio and Machine Workers of America

My name is Daniel Winters. I am president of Local 118, United Electrical, Radio and Machine Workers of America, Richmond, Indiana. I work at the Richmond Works of International Harvester. In appearing before the House Agriculture Committee today, I am representing UE District Council Nine....

The members of our union have a vital interest in the farmers of America. The farmers and their families constitute one of the basic sections of the American people and, representing 17% of the population, they consume all kinds of manufactured products made by our members. When the farmers are prosperous, it means that we, the workers, have full-time employment. And when the farmers suffer a decline in income, such as the 12% decline in the last year, it means that members of our union are without work and suffer all kinds of hardships. We represent thousands of workers in farm equipment plants where there have been serious layoffs because farmers are unable to pay the high prices of farm machinery....

Chapter 9

OVER LUNCH ANNA'S been listening to him expound on the male role, how men should share household responsibilities, think of marriage as a partnership. To a North American woman, he's probably saying all the right things. And demonstrating his sincerity by working in the kitchen alongside the two women, making a salad while she prepares the main course and their guest sets the table. Afterwards too, putting the dishes away after they've been washed and dried. No, it's not that he's hypocritical.

At the table, as he talks about men being little boys and woman as "special and exceptional," Anna's resentment festers. Throughout their marriage the pedestal has been omnipresent, so at hand that he's tripped over it a number of times, forgetting that the woman too has needs that can't be met as long as she's up there. Teetering, in fact. If she'd seen the problem earlier, if she'd refused to stand perched up there alone or insisted that he stand beside her, would things have been different? Would he have been there when she needed him?

You've often told your students, she says aloud, of your disdain for the Mexican macho image, and how important it is for a man to help with parenting and household responsibilities. But you're focusing on a task partnership, and a woman needs an emotional partner as well. You can't be her emotional partner if you've elevated her. As long as you see her as the eternal breast, you have need of her but are blind to the mutuality of need.

Humph, he says.

IN THE EARLY 1950s it was an unusual situation for Reid Memorial Hospital—a white woman giving birth to a child fathered by a black man. Tongues were wagging, nurses inquiring of the doctor, "What is it?" as though it were a mutation of two species. "Well, what does it look like?" Dr. Stevens grumbled. "It's a girl."

Daniel and Anna named her Carla.

Though not officially segregated, the hospital had non-articulated rules against putting black and white patients together. To have a white mother visited by the black father might be offensive to another white woman sharing the room. That she had a room to herself suited Anna fine.

Two years later, following the birth of Helena, Anna was placed with a white roommate. After the roommate's release, nurses carefully searched the mattress for bugs, then thoroughly cleaned it. Apparently they had paired Anna with someone who would be offensive to any *clean* white woman.

THINK OF THE CHILDREN. When and why did Americans begin to frame the issue of biracial marriage around the children?

In 1662 the colony of Virginia passed legislation declaring a child to be whatever its mother was. Except for Maryland, the other colonies followed suit. The white master who fathered children by a slave woman got more property. A male slave who fathered a child by a white woman might be punished by his master but usually he would not be lynched as black men were after the Civil War. He was, after all, someone's property, therefore of financial value.

Taboos didn't always work. In Maryland, the law required that a white woman who wanted to marry a black slave give up her freedom and the freedom of resulting children. Yet such marriages occurred anyway. Throughout the South black men and white women lived together as husband and wife without official sanction. In the North too, in states where biracial couples were forbidden to marry, the couple would move to a state where it was not illegal.

So the issue was reframed: *mixing the blood* became the problem. The word *mulatto* emerged as a term for children of black-white liaisons. (Etymologists aren't agreed on the origins of the word, though many believe it came from Spanish and Portuguese, meaning *mule*, that is the progeny of a horse and donkey.) The white race needed to be protected from being contaminated by inferior races. Many white scholars of the mid-nineteenth century argued that black people were of a different species.[32] Some claimed that mulattos could not reproduce for more than three generations, which meant their line was weakened by *mixing the blood.* Among neurologists there were some who claimed the body had electrical signals, that these signals flowed one direction in whites and another in blacks. Children born of one black parent and one white parent would be confused.[33] Racially mixed children would be "sickly, effeminate, and generally inferior."[34] The white race dare not allow itself to be contaminated.

In the late nineteenth century Jim Crow laws in the South imposed the separation of Negro and white, forcing the use of separate public facilities such as water fountains, restrooms, and train cars. But how could whites be sure who was a Negro? The solution: create the *one drop rule*; that is if a person had any trace of African ancestry (one drop), the person was a Negro.

What started in the South—an obsession with protecting the purity of white womanhood, a determination to keep the white race pure, and the idea that one drop of Negro blood made a person a Negro—didn't stay in just the South. These notions became entrenched in Northern thinking as well.

Think of the children, friends told Anna. They will not likely be accepted in the Negro or white community, and society will consider them Negroes.

Two movies of the 1930s, the period when Anna and her friends were going to movies, pointed to the tragedy that was sure to fall upon children of black-white liaisons.

In *Imitation of Life* (1934) Delilah (Louise Beavers), a black woman, and Bea (Claudette Colbert), a white woman, are widows with daughters. Delilah's fair-skinned daughter, Peola (Fredi Washington), who was most likely fathered by a white man, struggles with her identity as a Negro and avoids being seen with her dark mother. Years later as an adult, Peola breaks her mother's heart by choosing to pass as white. She is the film's tragic figure, a *mulatto* who cannot accept her black mother or her own race.

In *Showboat* (1936) a local sheriff comes aboard the showboat to arrest actors Julie and Steve on charges of miscegenation. The sheriff announces that Julie, who has been passing as white, is really the daughter of a black woman and a white man. While the story is mainly about Magnolia, daughter of the captain and his wife, it doesn't end without another glimpse of Julie, many years later. Abandoned by Steve and drinking heavily, she earns a living by singing in a night club. Again, the offspring of a racially mixed marriage is doomed to a life of sorrow.

IN THE BIG playhouse Daniel had built in the back yard, Helena was setting the table with little dishes, knives, and forks. She put the white knives and forks at one place and said, "Mommy will sit here." Placing the brown knives and forks opposite them, she said, "Daddy will sit here." To Anna's knowledge this was the first time either girl expressed an awareness of skin color.

Early on she'd recognized that talking with them about race would be as challenging as someday talking about sex. Keep the right balance, she told herself. Be honest without giving credence to society's attitudes.

The summer before Carla, the older of the two, entered kindergarten, Anna was driving the girls to the grocery. Standing behind the front seat of the car, on opposite sides (a common way for children to ride back then), the girls peered out at sights they passed.

Helena pointed. "Mommy, what's that?"

"That's a swimming pool."

"Can children go to a swimming pool?"

"Yes, some children swim at the pool."

"Can we go sometime?" Carla asked.

"No, sweetheart, I'm afraid they won't let you swim there."

"Why not?"

"Some people have made very mean rules about swimming pools. They've decided that only certain people can use them."

"But you said children can go to the swimming pool. We're children."

"Yes, but they only let in certain children."

"What do you mean?"

Anna pulled the car over to the curb and reached back to touch Helena's arm. "Well, look at what a beautiful, golden shade of brown your skin is. Some people have made a bad rule that says people with lovely brown skin can't swim at the pool. Isn't that a silly rule?"

"Daddy's skin is a lot browner than mine," Carla said. "They'll let Daddy swim there, won't they?"

"No, they won't. I'll tell you what, though, let's ask Daddy to put a big wash tub in our backyard, make our own swimming pool. How does that sound?"

"That doesn't sound like a good idea. Me and Helena can swim in a tub, but Daddy's too big. The pool people should let him in, because he needs a lot of room."

Helena said, "I think Daddy should go tell them to let him swim there."

"I have another idea," Anna said. "This Sunday all four of us will go to the lake. Where we can all swim."

"Yea," the girls chorused as Anna put the car back in gear.

Thoughts about skin color continued to race through Helena's mind. The day after the swimming pool conversation, instead of joining Carla in the sandbox, she hovered as Anna hung clothes on the line. "Mommy, why does Daddy have brown skin and you have white skin?"

Anna returned the pair of Daniel's work pants to the laundry basket and squatted to her daughter's level.

"Well, let's see if I can explain. You remember Grandma Pearl. She was Daddy's mother."

"Uh-huh."

"She had a grandmother once too. A long, long time ago. Grandma Pearl's grandma and grandpa came to our country from Africa, where people have dark brown skin. But they didn't leave Africa because they wanted to."

Anna noticed how intently Helena looked into her eyes, as if she too knew this was an important conversation and wanted to be sure she understood it all.

"Men captured them and put them on a ship and brought them across the ocean to America. When they got here, they were sold—just like you would sell a car or a washing machine—to someone who made them do all kinds of work. These people from Africa were called slaves. The people who owned them made them work very, very hard."

Helena placed her hands on her little hips and thrust her chest forward. "Well, I would have run away."

Anna: "I enjoyed motherhood. I didn't feel bored or imposed upon. Motherhood provided variety and satisfaction, seldom drudgery. For me those years when the girls were growing up were beautiful years. I was always excited by the idea that they would develop into women with their own identity."

Inez, Anna's closest college friend, later recalled that for a while she and her husband, a pastor, lived just over the state line in Ohio. When Anna, Daniel, and the girls visited, Inez couldn't help but notice Anna's commitment to motherhood, the way she never put adult interaction above the girls' needs, her loving tone of voice when she spoke with them. She believed that Anna's childhood losses made her determined to be the kind of mother she'd missed when growing up.

"I think she wanted more than anything to have a home, a real home," Inez said.

SOON AFTER RETURNING to Richmond, after living in Minneapolis, Anna had made two decisions regarding her relationship to Violet: first, she would not subject the man she loved to encounters in which civility was the most they could expect; second, if her family would not accept Daniel as a member, she would keep her distance.

Daniel: "We have a son-in-law whose mother was very opposed to our daughter and didn't welcome her in her home. He would leave our daughter and go visit his mother. Anna would never have done that. She said, 'If Daniel isn't invited, I'm not coming.' When we married she made it clear to her family: 'If you don't accept him, you can't accept me.' I've never lost sight of the fact that she was willing to give up her family for me, that just as she vowed at our wedding, she really did end up forsaking all others."

The week they learned Anna was pregnant with Carla, Daniel began adding a room to the house. Passing within a few blocks on the way to and from work would have been enough reason for most brothers-in-law to stop by to examine the progress, offer words of advice, perhaps even pitch in. But George, who had excellent carpentry skills and had turned the attic of his and Violet's house into two upstairs bedrooms, did not once come over. On the other hand, Henry, Joyce's nineteen-year-old boyfriend, spent hours hanging around, talking to Daniel as he worked, assisting when he could.

Perhaps it was the arrival of children that finally softened Violet's attitude toward the Winters family. Violet's daughter Myra wrote, "I have no clue how Mom became reconciled to Daniel. My guess would be that...by learning to know Daniel she felt better towards him. Who could resist him?"

Perhaps, too, Anna wanted her daughters to know their aunt and cousins, who now that they were teenagers took special delight in younger children. Sundays Violet and family took the girls to church. In spite of having severed ties to the Church of the Brethren, Anna wanted her daughters to be exposed to Christian values. The two families began to relate.

Years later, on more than one occasion, Violet and George visited Anna and Daniel in Mexico City. As Violet had decades earlier opened her home to the parentless child, Anna extended hospitality to her sister and brother-in-law.

IN THE 2000 CENSUS, for the first time, Americans identifying their race could check more than one box. Ten years later, the 2010 census showed that "The number of people of all ages who identified themselves as both white and black soared by 134 percent...to 1.8 million people."[35] Likely this boost in numbers doesn't represent more individuals as much as it reflects growing acceptance of being mixed-race. Our attitudes have changed so dramatically that in 2008 and 2012 we elected Barack Obama, a man born of an African father and a Caucasian mother, President.

However, it's likely that had Anna's and Daniel's daughters grown up in the United States, in Indiana, they would have experienced not only the type of prejudice their father lived with but also an additional form of racism: the sort reserved for children who were neither obviously black nor obviously white.

Chapter 10

*D*ANIEL AND NANCY *return from the supermercado a few blocks away, carrying expandable plastic net bags bulging with goods. Anna listens to her North American guest marvel over what for locals is a routine trip: the house next door condemned after the 1985 earthquake, the smells of the small, intimate restaurant a few doors away; the young mechanic who operates his business partly in the garage of a house, partly on the sidewalk; the grocery similar to ones in the U.S., except product names are in Spanish and there are fresh fruits and vegetables Nancy's never seen before.*

Anna, her back to the metal kitchen sink, hands spread out, gently clasping the curved edges, is bemused. Until Nancy tells about the encounter with two energetic elderly women who were obviously delighted to run into Daniel. Stepping away from the sink, Anna begins to unpack the groceries, allowing the refrigerator door to slam a little louder than she might otherwise. Closing the cupboard door with a little more force than usual. Yes, even in his seventies Daniel still has a way with women. His eyes sparkle and his grin welcomes.

The pain begins somewhere in an undefined part of Anna's core and spreads throughout her body. Muffling the guest's spirited conversation, she begins to scour the kitchen sink. Even though she did it only yesterday.

UNTIL INTERNATIONAL HARVESTER closed its Richmond plant in 1958, their marital roles had been similar to those of many households following the war: The husband provided for the family, the wife stayed home with the children. Daniel's involvement in the union had given him recognition and a sense of mission. Anna, deprived during most of her own childhood of a mother's presence, had found pleasure in full-time motherhood.

Now, with Daniel out of work and no prospects for a job, the couple spent hours at the kitchen table, adding columns of figures, Daniel telling Anna she needed to trim the household budget, she telling him she was already being as frugal as possible. Finally they agreed that the only option was for Anna to go to work, an alternative that appealed to neither of them. She would rather stay at home with the girls; he could only think of what her employment would say about his manhood. Besides, if she did search for a job, who in Richmond would hire a woman with the last name of Winters, a woman known to be married to a Negro, a communist Negro at that, maybe even one herself?

Combing the "Help Wanted" section of *The Palladium Item,* Anna read that the state mental hospital needed aides. If she could get a job on the night shift, she could be at home with the girls during the day. With some luck no one would care who an aide was married to.

A former administrator herself, she had sat on the opposite side of the desk interviewing dozens, if not hundreds, of job applicants. Now, seated across from the personnel director and in desperate need to a job, she felt nervous. Was the belted brown and white striped cotton dress, skirt cut on the bias, the right attire? Did her bearing convey just the right degree of compassion and competence, neither too little nor too much?

The personnel director, barely looking at her, had taken the application and nodded for Anna to have a seat. For what felt like an interminable amount of time, the woman's attention remained focused on the piece of paper. Anna imagined her thinking *Winters, Winters, why does that name ring a bell?* Then she'd figure out and laugh at the audacity of this commie sympathizer thinking someone would give her a job.

"It says here you have a college degree and that in the past you've had some very responsible jobs as a social worker," the woman said. "Why are you applying for a position as an aide?"

Without giving Anna a chance to answer, the director continued. "We need a social worker right now." For the first time she looked up to meet Anna's gaze. "Why don't you apply for that position?" Apparently the Winters name meant nothing to her, nor to the newly appointed administrator who immediately interviewed the applicant and hired her.

By the time it was drawn to management's attention that the new social worker was the wife of one of the town's leading malcontents, and a black man at that, Anna had already been on the job two weeks. She could tell by the way administrators looked the other way when she walked by that had they known who her husband was, they would have made certain her application landed on the rejection pile.

Years later Daniel acknowledged that her working affected their relationship more than they realized at the time. He didn't mind being at home. In fact, spending time with the girls, preparing their lunches, putting them down for their naps, probably contributed to the closeness the three of them would always feel. But watching his wife go out the door each day reminded him of his failure to be a good provider.

FOR A FEW months Anna convinced herself that their commitment to tell each other what was on their mind was an agreement more in principle than in fact. Besides, she was confident she could handle the situation. If she told Daniel he'd worry. No, he'd be furious; the anger that constantly simmered within him would erupt. On the other hand, if it were the other way around—if Daniel were the one confronted daily with such uncomfortable situations—she'd want to know.

On an evening in spring she waited until supper dishes were washed, the girls in bed. "I need to talk with you," she said, taking his hand and leading him into the living room. On the sofa, still clinging tightly to his hand, she turned to face him so she could study his eyes, see his reaction.

"I want you to know about some things at work. I don't want you to worry. I can handle it." She paused to clear her throat. "At work the doctors talk like monogamous relationships are out of fashion. They tell each other—I'll be right in the room, and they act like I'm not there. No, I'm sure it's because I *am* there—they tell each other about their sexual exploits. With a lot of detail."

Daniel's usually expressive eyes were unreadable. Was he even listening to her? She continued. "And if they're alone with me—they don't touch me or anything like that—we can be in the middle of a conversation about a certain patient, and they'll find a way to relate it to sex. They're not even subtle. I've been trying to figure out how to respond. To laugh and act as though they're joking seems to be inviting more of the same, but to tell them I'm offended—that would jeopardize my job." His continued lack of response led her to go beyond what she'd planned to say. "What I can't figure out is why they're acting this way. Do they assume that if I sleep with a colored man, I must have liberal views about sex?"

Daniel stood and walked to the window. She went to his side and put her arm around his waist. Though darkness had started to blanket the world beyond their living room, they hadn't yet pulled down the blinds.

"Maybe it's their way of getting me to quit."

The wind was blowing whirlybirds fallen from the maple trees in front of the house, lifting them, swirling them around, dropping them on the front porch. Up and down the block lamps from the homes of neighbors, nearly everyone a Negro, cast shadows on window shades.

She already regretted telling Daniel about her problems at work. Compared to what he'd endured on the job, what their neighbors coped with every day, her problems were miniscule. No, that wasn't true. Daniel should understand as well as anyone what it was like to be the recipient of hostile remarks, for that's what they were. Not an affirmation of her femininity but a rebuff, hostility that implied she wasn't worth the doctors' respect.

Daniel faced her and pulled her close, wrapping his arms around her, burying his face in her hair. "It's all my fault, Sweetheart. If I was working you wouldn't have to spend each day in the company of vulgar men." She couldn't see his face but knew: the energetic eyes that had first attracted her had gone dull. He wasn't worried; he wasn't angry. His ego was punctured.

NEARLY TWENTY-FIVE YEARS had passed since Daniel had graduated from college. As he looked back on those years he recalled the private monotony of pushing brooms and running machinery; the public stimulation of making speeches on behalf of the union and representing it to the community. But when he reached even further into his past he discovered faint yet satisfying memories of standing in front of a classroom.

Mrs. Johnson, his student teaching supervisor, had often remarked that he was a born teacher. Seldom, she said, had she seen a young college student stand before a class with that level of poise, and when he'd taught adult education for the WPA, his students, all of them white, had responded positively. With teaching had come legitimate authority and respect, two remunerations a Negro man didn't usually get. Already forty-eight years old, he assumed it was too late to begin a new career. But the thought kept returning: except for student teaching and his brief WPA job, he had never been able to do what as a young man he had prepared for, that is teach Spanish.

Finally he brought Anna into his sphere of thought. If he did decide to try teaching, he wondered aloud, had he forgotten most of the Spanish he'd learned almost twenty-five years ago? Would his mind still be able to absorb new information? She encouraged him to audit a few Spanish classes at Earlham. The excitement of studying another language, another culture, returned. The vocabulary returned. Anna was elated by what she saw happening to him. The new challenges enlivened him, quickened his step, inspired him to swing her in his arms.

His mother had always pushed him to aspire and had never accepted any excuses for a job half done. Do not allow others or circumstances to limit your dreams for the future, she had taught him. Be the best. He knew that to be the best he needed more intensive language training.

SUPPER WAS OVER, the remaining food still on the table in serving bowls, both girls' plates clean except for green beans pushed to the side. Helena and Carla went into the living room to play dolls; Anna carried two cups of coffee from the stove over to the table. As she sat down Daniel reached over and pushed a stray lock out of her face.

"We need to talk something over." He brought the sugar bowl to his cup, stirring in two spoonsful. "I've been thinking that if I'm going to become a good Spanish teacher, I need practice speaking Spanish. After class today I hung around and talked to Dr. Stevens about what she recommends. She spoke very highly of the master's degree that Mexico City University offers."

"Mexico City!?" Not even Anna knew whether she was asking a question or making an exclamation.

"Darling, believe me, I wish Spanish was Indiana's official language. Look at it this way, Mexico's closer than Spain."

"Are you thinking you'd go alone, or that we'd all go?"

"I don't know."

From the next room came the shouts of an argument. Anna rose to intervene.

"They can settle it," Daniel said. She sat back down.

"How long would it take to get the degree?" she finally asked.

"Probably a year, maybe a little longer."

"A year," she repeated quietly. "If we went with you, how would we make it financially?"

"That'd be one of the problems. It'd be cheaper if I went alone. I'd just rent a room somewhere. And come back for vacations."

Her mind was racing, trying to solve several problems at once. "If the girls and I stay here, I could keep working, and Carla could continue with school. It would probably be less unsettling for them to stay here." She reached over to touch his arm. "This really is important to you, isn't it?"

"Yes, but I'm not sure it's important enough to go alone. We've got time to think it over. Tomorrow I'll write to the school for information. It'll probably be easier to make a decision when we know more."

ALTHOUGH HE HAD mastered two languages, Daniel regretted that he could not adequately put into words his immediate love for Mexico.

"Until I came here, I had no idea of the freedom you have experienced all your life," he wrote home in the fall of 1957. "I can go into any hotel, any restaurant. No one looks at me as though I have no right to be there. People treat me just like they treat everyone else."

Daniel: "I remember very clearly walking down the street and thinking, this is Paradise. No one looked at me with a surly expression. When I entered a store, the clerks didn't wait on everyone else first. It took me a little while to overcome the self-consciousness that resulted from my never having been allowed in nice hotels and restaurants.

"I came to Mexico because of the possibilities Anna gave me. If it hadn't been for her working, I wouldn't have been able to come. She sent me fifty dollars every month for my room and board and never once complained, never even insinuated that she resented doing this. So I had no qualms about being here. I felt I was going to school for her too and when I was finished, my education would be for the two of us."

DANIEL HAD BEEN gone less than a month when Elmer Hopkins dropped by the house. To see Daniel he said, but everyone who knew Daniel knew he was in Mexico. After that Elmer stopped by a few times each week, sometimes with little gifts for the girls, sometimes with a bottle of wine. Then he began coming later, after the girls were in bed.

Anna had invited a young couple, friends of Daniel's oldest son, for dinner one evening. The girls were in bed, and the three adults were visiting in the living room when Elmer arrived at the door, carrying a bottle of wine. What his appearance suggested to the couple, Anna could only guess. They said it was time to leave; she encouraged them to stay longer, aware, though, that her words sounded like a deception. They left and Elmer stayed late.

The following weekend he called from Indianapolis, trying to make arrangements for them to spend the weekend together. She was not interested, she told him emphatically.

Again she was faced with what to tell Daniel. She didn't want him to worry, but it was important that he know what was going on. The letter she finally composed sounded light-hearted. "Can you believe that stupid Elmer?" she wrote in the first paragraph.

"I think, Darling," Daniel responded in his next letter, "if we review all the things we have gone through and the way we have survived them, there should be no question about our future. Anna, Honey, how important it is to know that there have been no silly relationships to mar our being together again. I feel so lucky to have someone like you. To be frank, Darling, you have surprised me a little. I have confidence in you, but I know how designing people can be and how easily one can innocently be drawn into their contrivances. I trusted your intentions but I had concern about your—shall I label it inexperience? You always give people the benefit of the doubt. I don't think you would deliberately enter into anything, so I'm sure we could reconcile and not let it affect our relationship. You are, Little Flower, as I've always said, wonderful. So Darling, nothing—nothing can ever come between us."

THE NORTH AMERICAN Cultural Institute offered conversation classes for Mexican students wanting to learn English. It was through the Institute, where Daniel often went to help students practice English, that he met Sergio, Amelio, and Mario. The three men, all in their mid-twenties, became his friends.

On New Year's Day he accompanied them to the race track, a pastime which he later learned was more compatible with single than with family life. All day long it rained such a cold, chilling drizzle that his body became stiff and sore. Returning to his room, he wrapped himself in several blankets and put his feet in a tub of warm water. Unable to recall having ever been colder, he spent the night, teeth chattering, cursing any country that didn't have adequate heating systems.

Yet the next day he wrote a long letter to Anna. "One of my main thoughts is that in Mexico our daughters wouldn't have to suffer the racial discrimination that I and my other children have had to endure. I hope that as you think this over, Anna, you'll see how wonderful a move here could be for our family. All my love, Daniel."

For the three months he had been gone she often wondered how long it would be before he suggested moving. It was clear from his very first letter that he was happy in Mexico. More than happy; he felt free.

When they had talked of getting married, she'd often thought that a move to another country might solve some of the problems of a biracial marriage. Why live in a society that didn't accept them? The idea, which had seemed like an adventure back then, still had its appeal. She wrote back an enthusiastic yes.

Meanwhile, despite his instant affection for Mexico, Daniel was disappointed in the university's Spanish program. Classmates were mostly from the United States and spoke English outside of class. Already he felt at home and wanted to be with his new compatriots. After one *trimestre* he changed to the National University of Mexico, where his academic and social life became centered around the people and language of the country.

CHOICES, CHOICES, CHOICES. Life had been reduced to choices, Anna mused as she stood in the middle of the living room. What did she have that couldn't be purchased in Mexico? What toys or personal items would help the girls adjust to a new home? What could she absolutely not do without? The beautiful antique dishes that had belonged to Daniel's mother—she certainly couldn't sell those. But it would be foolish to use precious space in their small trailer for something that wasn't essential.

There were boxes of mementos she couldn't bring herself to throw away, ones that contained every letter and poem Daniel had ever written to her. Daniel, who was even more sentimental than she, had saved sports ribbons, programs, newspaper articles, and all the letters she'd ever written him. She decided to leave books and boxes of mementos with Violet, the antique dishes with Daniel's cousin. Someday, probably within the next few years, they'd come back for another load.

But it would be 1981, twenty-three years, before they would be able to take the rest of their possessions to Mexico. Meantime, the boxes kept changing location. When Daniel's cousin moved into a trailer, he asked Violet to put the dishes in her attic. Several years later, when Violet and George sold their house and retired to Florida, they gave everything to Daniel's daughter by his first marriage, who miraculously fit her father's and Anna's belongings into the small house occupied by her ten-member family.

Like many others who have sorted through belongings in preparing to move, Anna later realized that some of her decisions were mistakes. Settled in her new home, she often imagined discovering her old washing machine out on the patio and embracing it.

Daniel had returned home in March, 1958, assuming it would be a simple task to sell the house and pack up the few necessary belongings, but finding a buyer for the house was difficult. Finally a man who knew they were anxious to be off offered a ridiculously low price, which, in desperation, they accepted. Yet they anticipated that the money from the sale of the house, plus income Anna earned (assuming she could find work), would support them until Daniel got his degree.

It was August before the family was able to leave Richmond. All the belongings they thought they would need in their new life were loaded into a 1953 Ford station wagon and a small trailer.

HELENA SHIFTED HER body and lodged a bony little shoulder into her mother's thigh. Trying to give her more room, Anna twisted and sought a new position. As they had done other nights, the family had parked along the roadside, Daniel and Carla sleeping in the front seat that extended all the way across the car, Anna and Helena in the back. Anna adjusted the pillow between her head and the window. Soon she found herself wide awake. Through the partially open windows could be heard the clicks of insects, the haunting hoot of an owl.

She changed position, sitting up straight, repositioning Helena's head so both of them would be more comfortable. She peered out the front window into a night so devoid of light that it was impossible to know the nature of the surrounding landscape. In the distance two beams, no doubt the lights of a vehicle, broke through the blackness. Closer and closer they came, until she was positive it was a truck. And that it was heading straight for their car. She let out a piercing scream. Daniel and the girls bolted to alert sitting positions as the truck, following the road's curve to the right, thundered on into the night. Anna put her hand to her rapidly beating heart for several seconds before she burst out laughing.

They traveled several more days than they had anticipated in temperatures they had heard about but never before experienced. (This was, of course, before the ordinary car had air-conditioning.) At meal time they picnicked along the side of the road. In spite of the heat and the length of the journey, the girls, ages five and seven, proved to be good travelers.

On August 28, 1958, the Winter family arrived at the border. "Here we are—Mexico!" Daniel announced as he pulled the car to a stop in front of a *caseta*, a small inspection house. He leaned over to kiss Anna on the cheek.

"Here we are, girls," she said, "the country that will be our new home." Although Mexico City was still five hundred miles away, she felt as if they'd already accomplished a great feat.

Twenty miles further. More stops at more *casetas*, where each time they were asked to present their papers. Then another stop, and a border guard who seemed to take his official status quite earnestly, examining their papers more thoroughly, asking questions, questions, questions. Daniel and Anna grew increasingly nervous.

This was the situation: Had Daniel been able to return to Mexico within three months of his trip home, he could have reentered on his student papers. However, selling the house and preparing for such a big move had taken more than three months, which necessitated his reapplying for student status. Day after day he or Anna had walked out to the mailbox, desperate for the papers' arrival. If they didn't come soon, the family wouldn't have enough time to get settled before the next *trimestre* began. Finally, Daniel decided they would enter the country with tourist papers. (His new student papers arrived ten days after they left Richmond.)

"I see you have tourist papers," this border guard observed. "What are you planning to do while you're in Mexico?" He was closely scrutinizing the car and trailer, obviously loaded down with more than camping gear and suitcases.

"I'm going to study," Daniel answered.

"You can't study on tourist papers."

"I was studying in Mexico City before. Here are my student papers. They've expired, but they show that I've been a student here."

"Mr. Winters, do you realize you are breaking the law? You have two sets of papers here."

"No, I only have one set. The student papers have expired."

The guard kept insisting that Daniel was breaking the law. Daniel kept insisting he was not, pausing every now and then to translate what was going on to Anna. From the backseat the girls complained that it was hot and asked *Why aren't we going?* Daniel was more often the one who lost his temper, but this time Anna's patience ran out. She reached across Daniel and snatched the papers from the guard's hand.

She learned her first lesson about life in Mexico: No one, especially a woman, gets by with grabbing anything out of an official's hands. The guard insisted they drive the twenty miles back to the border. To make sure they followed his orders he sent along a police escort on a motorcycle.

The hot August air was so suffocating they couldn't decide whether it was more comfortable to keep the car windows open or closed. Anna was berating herself for having been so rash as to grab the papers, and Daniel was wondering whether they might have been better off had he not shown the guard his student papers. The girls kept interrupting both their thoughts with anxious questions about why they had to have this policeman on a motorcycle go with them. Had they done something bad? Were they going to jail?

They were crossing a double railroad track at Reynosa, when the girls' questions were interrupted by a clang followed by the loud sound of metal scraping the road. The car lurched. While it continued moving forward, the trailer remained on the tracks. The hitch had broken.

The police escort immediately recruited a few onlookers to pull the trailer off the tracks. With a tone of urgency and authority he then dispatched one of them to go in search of a welder. While they waited, Anna and the girls sought relief from the heat in the shadow of a small stucco building.

Fifteen minutes, twenty, half an hour passed without any sign of the welder. Certain the runner had never delivered the message, Daniel suggested to their escort that someone else be sent. The officer said it wouldn't be necessary; the welder would come.

It may have been that the police officer grew tired of standing out in the sun. Or that he needed to take a leak and was afraid that if he left, Daniel would pile the family back in the car and miraculously pull the trailer back toward Mexico City. Without revealing his reason or destination, he insisted that Daniel accompany him down the unpaved intersecting road. Looking over at Anna and the girls standing by the building, Daniel knew he couldn't walk off with this man and abandon them. He refused to leave. The officer threatened to put him in jail.

Not understanding Spanish, Anna didn't know what was happening, only that the officer was being insistent. She could tell by Daniel's tone of voice, the firmness of his jaw, the bulging veins in his neck that he was making every effort to control his temper.

From a whirlwind of dust a handcart appeared. It was the welder, a good-natured man pulling along the equipment he needed. While a group of men stood around, looking on and visiting with the welder, he repaired the trailer hitch.

Perhaps it was sympathy for this family whose arrival in Mexico was not going well; perhaps it was time for the officer to go off duty. Whatever his motive, Daniel and Anna were surprised when he suggested that they turn around and head back south without him. He assured them there would be no problems when they returned to the *caseta* of the official who had ordered them to return to the border. They weren't sure they could believe a man who a short time earlier had been threatening to put Daniel in jail, but given the choices, they decided to do as he said. They turned around and headed in the direction of Mexico City. Much to their relief, when they arrived back at the checkpoint, the obstinate official was gone and the new guard allowed them to pass through. By now it was late in the afternoon.

At about five o'clock they came to the final border inspection station. Since the chief was no longer on duty, according to the guards, Daniel and Anna would have to wait there until the next morning. Also, the guards explained, when the chief did arrive, he would insist that they unload the trailer and the car. While contemplating the challenge of unloading and reloading what had taken a week to pack, Daniel was also thinking that certainly the chief inspector couldn't be there all the time. Aha, he suddenly understood: they expected a bribe. After he handed them fifty pesos, one of the men loosened a flap of the tarpaulin, took a cursory glance, and said, "Pass on through."

A YEAR EARLIER, when checking a bulletin board for a place to live, Daniel had come upon Casa de huespedes, which Señora Palacios had just opened on Chapultepec. Glad to have his American dollars, the señora had treated him as a special boarder. Upon the family's arrival in Mexico City, he drove directly to the rooming house. "How fortunate," Señora Palacios said, "the student who has been renting your old room is on vacation. Your family can stay there until you find a place to live."

Anna didn't mind that the family would have to share the bathroom down the hall or that the room had only one narrow bed, a dresser, and a small table with a single chair. She did mind, however, that dirty clothes were strewn everywhere, the sheets were gray, and food residue and mold were on the windowsills and table. In no time she and Daniel had stuffed the clothes in the narrow closet, along with the sheets, and scrubbed every surface. The blankets they'd put atop the contents of the car were spread on the floor for the girls to sleep on. After nights of sharing the back seat of the car with Helena, a single bed for two seemed almost a luxury.

It was their third night, about two o'clock in the morning. All four Winters were into a sound slumber, faint snores emanating from Daniel's mouth. The door of the room opened, not with the faint creak of stealth but with a bold clamor of entry. The silhouette of a large man wearing a sombrero appeared in the doorway. "Quien es?" Daniel shouted as he bolted upright. Anna gasped; the girls whimpered.

The intruder was as startled as they were. It was his room. After Daniel stepped out into the hall and explained that Señora Palacios hadn't expected him back for several days, the young man went down the hall to the room of a friend. The following day Daniel and Anna found a pleasant second-floor, two-bedroom apartment.

Anna immediately set about getting the girls situated in school. To her North American way of thinking, the family would become more a part of their new country by attending public schools. She soon learned, however, that the public schools provided a minimal education to the masses, whereas parents who wanted their children to be well educated, if they could afford it, sent them to private schools.

However, there was a shortage of private schools, their philosophies varied, and some were better than others. Methodical and thorough in her search, Anna traveled the section of the city closest to their apartment, looking for the right educational setting. Not knowing Spanish, she tried day after day to communicate to taxi drivers which school she wanted to be taken to. From the back seat she and the girls gazed with curiosity at this large, colorful city that was their new home.

She wrote to Carla's first grade teacher in Indiana, asking for advice. Would repeating first grade help Carla adjust to the culture and language? Or would she likely become bored and lose interest in learning? Upon the teacher's advice, she decided to place Carla in second grade and eliminate from her list those schools that were highly structured or seemed to have little free activity.

They checked out the American School, where the girls played well with the children and had a delightful time. If enrolled there, they would receive instruction in Spanish but could continue their studies in English. It was considered an excellent academic institution, but the tuition was high, and besides, she didn't want her daughters to be part of the American community. At the conclusion of careful research, she decided to send them to a small school near their apartment, but what was supposed to be a strong academic program turned out to be disappointing.

In a letter to Violet she wrote that it broke her heart when the girls cried to go back to Indiana. They missed their friends and the house and yard. At night Helena woefully sang a little song she made up about wanting to be "home in Richmond."

And there was the matter of money. They had made their plans to move assuming they would get a fair price for their house. Now they were forced to live on a thousand dollars less than they'd budgeted for the period Daniel would be studying, a large amount by Mexican standards. He was able to earn a little by teaching night classes in English, but it wasn't enough. Twice Anna had to swallow her pride and write to Violet and George, asking for a loan.

"I'm trying to keep my sense of values in balance," she wrote them. "The roots and security we had in having a home don't make it easy to accept giving everything up. What one has within oneself, emotional security—the way one uses knowledge—can't be lost. That is all we have now."

As she'd always been, Anna remained optimistic, adventuresome. She stayed convinced that this move to Mexico was going to open a whole new world for her family.

"WE ARE IN TROUBLE," Anna wrote to Violet and George less than a year after their arrival in Mexico. Their car had to be registered in Mexico City and the permit renewed on a regular basis. With the expiration date approaching, Daniel arrived at the *registro* to discover the office was closed for a week. The following week he made three more trips, each time finding the doors of the facility locked. One of those times he arrived just as the office was closing. Personnel told him they would reopen in the afternoon, but when he went back, no one was there.

The following Monday, as he was returning to the *registro*, a car with a government insignia pulled him over—to point out a flat tire or something of that sort, he assumed. Instead, two men approached the car and pulled out credentials showing they were from the Hacienda Gobernacion.

"Señor, you are driving on an expired permit."

"Yes, I know. In fact, I was on my way to the *registro* right now."

"Okay, you can follow us back."

"Can I renew my permit then?"

"Oh, yes. *No hay problema.*"

Upon his arrival at the *registro*, guards opened the gates and motioned for him to drive inside. There an official led him into a small office and asked a score of seemingly irrelevant questions: When did he purchase the car? Where? What did he use it for? Where did he drive it each day? When the officer had recorded Daniel's answers, he led him down a long hallway to another office, where he presented the papers to a man seated at a desk.

"Señor Winters, is this information correct?" the second official asked, peering over reading glasses.

"Si." Nothing was said for a few moments as the officer stamped the papers with multitudinous seals in as many colors.

"To get your car back you'll have to go upstairs to see the chief."

Get his car *back?* Daniel soon learned that it had been impounded and that the cost of ransom was 92,000 pesos. He had purchased the '53 Ford station wagon for $795, the equivalent of about 10,000 pesos at that time.

"Are you Cuban?" the chief asked.

"No, I'm a North American."

"Well, I suggest you go to the American Embassy and get their help in working out this problem."

Venting his anger would only exacerbate the situation, Daniel knew, so he said a quick "Gracias, señor," and went directly to the American Embassy.

The man at the Protective Division was about Daniel's age and talked as though he had been in Mexico a long time. "To be honest, I don't understand what's going on. Usually, when things of this sort happen, it's an affair of Mexico, and we don't meddle in it. But since they sent you here—well, maybe they want to arrange it in a friendly manner. I'll see what I can do." Daniel returned home convinced he had let the family down.

The next day the Protective Division sent a lawyer over to the police department, but nothing came of the visit. As Daniel became even more discouraged, Anna vacillated between trying to boost his spirits and feeling homesick for a country where she understood the language and procedures.

When he mentioned his problem at school, a fellow student said his cousin worked at the *registro*. He'd take care of it. *No hay problema.* But after his cousin had seen the chief, the student came to Daniel and said accusingly, "You went to the American Embassy."

"Yes, I did."

"Why?"

"Well, they sent me."

"I can't do anything now, because it would appear that the United States government was putting pressure on the Mexican government. If you hadn't gone to the embassy we could have done something *abaja de lagua*" (under the table).

Another student knew a lawyer who could help. *No hay problema,* the lawyer told Daniel.

In the meantime the status of their tourist papers was causing more anxiety. Because visitors with tourist papers could only remain in Mexico for a limited time, the family was required every six months to make the long journey up to the border, cross into the States, then reenter. Having arrived in Mexico with a car, they had to leave with a car. They didn't have the car. So they couldn't leave Mexico. But they couldn't stay in Mexico either.

Very quickly the lawyer friend of another student arranged for papers allowing them to leave and reenter Mexico without the car. "When you return, we'll work on getting it back," he promised. He did work on it for a while, but finally Daniel and Anna realized they were wasting precious money. They accepted the fact: they weren't going to get their car back.

Later, Daniel often caught sight of someone driving the station wagon he was certain belonged to them. One day, seeing it parked on the corner by Woolworth's, he decided to wait nearby and see who the driver was. Half an hour later a man in a uniform approached and started to get in the car.

"*Un momento.* I'd like to know how much you paid for this car." Daniel spoke in a curious, friendly manner.

"It's not my car. I just use it for my work at the Treasury Department. It's a car that was confiscated from a tourist for an infraction of the law."

"Yeah, I know," Daniel replied. "That's my car."

Acquaintances explained to him that in Mexico this sort of incident was not uncommon. Officials would spot a good foreign car, wait to see if there was any possibility of an infraction, then take it.

Without the car, trips to the border—at first by train, later by bus— became more difficult and expensive. Not until 1975 did they finally get permanent papers, and that was with the help of their son-in-law's father. In the meantime, they had obtained a temporary *visa de trabajo,* which gave foreigners permission to work and only required going to the border every two years.

Somewhere between the pressures of trying to get the girls settled, the loss of the car, and the dispute over papers, Anna's anticipation of adventure turned to feelings of disappointment and loneliness. This new life wasn't turning out as she had expected. In the United States Daniel often spoke of how he'd been treated as an unwelcome foreigner, how people assumed, just by looking at the color of his skin, that he was ignorant and dishonest. Although she had listened with an empathy deeply grounded in her love for him, and though in her own life she'd known what it felt like not to belong, she had never understood what it really was like to be a permanent outsider. Now she was experiencing—by choice, not by history, she kept reminding herself—something quite similar to what Daniel had endured his whole life. She was a fair-skinned woman in a country of dark complexions; an English-speaking woman in a Spanish-speaking land; a reserved, non-effusive woman amidst a demonstrative culture where emotions were often unrestrained.

Daniel was already a Mexican; she recognized she could never be.

Chapter 11

*L*OOKING OVER AT Daniel, Anna is aware of how long the green sofa is, of the small tape recorder resting on the center cushion, its microphone perched on a slim black plastic stand, capturing the details of her life. All of this—the sofa length, the recorder, a childhood that drew her inward yet opened her to others—it all seems confusing right now. She wants there to be nothing between her and Daniel, to nestle in the crook of his arm and gaze up at him. The way she did—so long ago it was.

Though small, the tape recorder's presence seems colossal, amplifying her history, pulling in the sound of her voice, magnetically clinging to words that are her life. How far apart she and Daniel sit on the long green sofa, how very far apart.

How could he have forgotten what it was like to be an outsider?

Of course he can't understand the deep sense of loss that comes with having no family, his own mother having been a dominant force in his life. Pearl had such high aspirations for her son that he believed he could accomplish whatever he set his mind to. Her sacrifices provided him with more than an education; she convinced him he was capable of forging an environment rather than of being forged by it.

Yet he understood what it was like not to belong. Even though he and Pearl remained close as long as she lived and he knew he belonged to the little family she had created for the two of them, he had to go out into the world each day. Society, which constantly worked against his mother, insisted he could expect to become nothing more than a janitor. Society would not let him forget he was an outsider, too.

How could he have forgotten what the two of them once shared?

"HOW'D YOUR DAY GO?" were always Daniel's first words of greeting upon entering the kitchen and kissing Anna on the cheek.

After graduating with his master's degree from the National University of Mexico, he had immediately found a job teaching English as a Second Language at a small private school run by an

American and a Mexican. For the first time in his life, he had a professional job. With it came respect and esteem.

Had Anna been one to cry more easily, tears might have relieved the tension and answered her husband's question better than words. He used to know her well enough to recognize every trace of pain. Lately, however, his own excitement over the new teaching job had catapulted him into a realm that was more Mexican than North American, more free than restrained, more separate from her than complementary.

"Oh, the usual." Her hands moved with expertise over the potatoes, meticulously searching out each disfiguring eye. "Whatever happened to the days when girls were made of sugar and spice and everything nice?" She was referring to the teenagers who resisted her efforts to teach them English. "If it were at all possible for the human body to hang suspended from the ceiling, those girls would be up there." A faint attempt at a laugh came from deep in her throat. "How about you?" Briskly she moved the cleaned potatoes from the tin bowl to a pan on top of the stove.

"Great. My day was great." He leaned against the doorjamb, holding the glass of orange juice he'd poured for himself. "The boys are already making progress. I worked them hard, then in each class we spent the last fifteen minutes discussing boy-girl relationships. They always like that."

To a mound of ground beef Anna added an egg, seasonings, and oatmeal. Reaching deep into the bowl, her fingers deftly blended the mixture.

"They all had to express their opinions in English, though," Daniel said. "I'd forgotten what it was like to be a boy that age, to have all those hormones so anxious to get out of control."

Stepping over to the sink, he began to empty the drainer of the morning's washed dishes. As he moved from one small cupboard to another, he went on to describe an interesting discussion on politics he'd had with the American-hating mathematics teacher.

It would have been a joy to see him happy had she not felt so wretched. He was in a country where he belonged, in the vocation where he belonged. Her life had no parallel joys.

Soon after moving to Mexico, she had come to accept the reality that her language deficiencies prevented her from ever becoming a social worker. Reconciling herself to the prospect of teaching English as a second language, she'd earned a certificate at the North American Cultural Institute for Training, where she met the director of a school for girls. He offered her a job teaching.

It turned out to be an overwhelming experience. Her skills were in listening to people and determining how to help them, not in controlling forty rambunctious girls at a time. Males of the species were capable of disruptive behavior, she'd always known, but girls too? Sensitive as she was to people's problems, accepting as she was of practically every kind of anomaly in human behavior, she could not excavate, even from her vast store of compassion, any appreciation for these adolescent females.

She was miserable.

Added to her stress was dissatisfaction over Carla's and Helena's academic program. Disappointed in the school they'd been attending, she'd transferred them to her school only to see firsthand the poor quality of education they were receiving. They weren't happy and she wasn't happy, and when evening came, she didn't have the energy to make it all up to them.

But at each day's end, the man of the house arrived, exuberant.

DANIEL HAD ALREADY made several acquaintances prior to the family's joining him. As Anna confronted her new life, searching for a school for the girls, and probing the possibilities for employment, she discovered a few friends of her own.

The family had been in the apartment on Rio Mississippi about two weeks when she stood downstairs in the building entry trying to explain to a man from the electric company that there was a problem with the meter. Unable to make her few words of Spanish comprehendible, she began to repeat what she'd already said, only louder. The blank look on the electrician's face made it clear she wasn't making any progress.

She laughed and shrugged her shoulders. He laughed and shrugged his shoulders. At about that time a man who had, even from his third-floor apartment, heard her shouting, came down the stairs and asked in English, "Can I be of help?" With his assistance, the electrician fixed the meter. The neighbor introduced himself as Fernando. His wife, Gloria, who was from the States, taught at the American School. They became Anna's good friends.

Early on, before she'd given up on finding a job as a social worker, she'd gone to see Margaret Waltersdorf, Director of Nursing at the American Hospital. The two women, who took an instant liking to each other, had daughters the same age. Margaret invited the Winters over for dinner, and a friendship that survived the decades began.

But friendships became a source of conflict between Anna and Daniel. In spite of wanting to become part of Mexican culture, she had trouble learning Spanish. This frustration, added to all the others, led her to gravitate toward people who spoke English. Daniel, though, found something wrong with every friend she had. Fernando was too bombastic, a dreamer who could talk plenty about his plans but never follow through. Margaret's husband was too passive.

Looking back over his life, Daniel recognized a counterfeit quality to his relationships. Survival in school or work had required the ability to make friends with whites, but inclusion in the life of the black community dictated that he be friends with his neighbors and not too tight with whites. While years of working at blue-collar jobs made him aware of the intelligence and integrity of the people he worked with, he considered his education and viewpoints as separating him from most of them. Weary from being nice to people he didn't like, being a friend to people who weren't quite his peers, he made up his mind that in Mexico he would only make friends with whomever he wished. He would be Mexican and have only Mexican friends.

Invariably social occasions that took the two of them into the homes of Anna's friends ended with the couple arguing all the way back to their apartment. She accused him of having been rude; he argued that he shouldn't have to be sociable when he really didn't care if he ever saw the people again. Wasn't it enough that she needed the friendship of these people? Couldn't he be pleasant for just these few hours—for her sake? No, he answered.

In bed those nights she was overcome by a longing for the way things used to be. She'd been attracted to Daniel's charming manner, the comfortable way he met people, his easy conversation. She'd seen him operate in the union, working for unity among the workers, always having a sound political sense. Where was the Daniel she knew and loved? Where was the Daniel who loved her enough to sacrifice for her happiness?

Anna: "Before we moved here I met refugees who had come to the United States from Europe. Groups sponsoring them tried to pave the way. People were interested and cared about helping them. When Daniel was here alone, people encouraged him to move the family here. They said, 'Come.' I thought we'd be helped the way the European refugees had been helped. I expected people to be more understanding about the language. Daniel felt so good about the freedom for him here that all the complications didn't seem important to him.

"I've been able to work some of these feelings out. But I grew up in a country that was home, and this is not home. Also, I grew up in a small town. This is a city. Life in the provinces is different. People are united, and they help each other more. When we came to Mexico City there were three and a half million people; now there are close to eighteen million. I expected our life here to be different than it's been. Maybe it's all my fault that things turned out as they did."

Daniel: "But you haven't had a normal life. If you'd married a white man, you wouldn't have run into the obstacles you've had to face. You wouldn't have had to leave the U.S. You would have been secure and satisfied."

Anna: "Of course, it would have been different. But I didn't want that."

Daniel: "I know you didn't." He chuckled.

HALFWAY INTO THE year, the American who was part owner of the school where Daniel taught took off to Peru, leaving full administrative responsibility with his Mexican partner. Friendly, accessible to teachers, the man was, however, inept in the financial aspects of managing a school. Finally money became such a serious problem that teachers went home on payday without a check, and the director, unable to face his staff, began spending more and more time away. The school year closed with far fewer students and teachers than when it started.

Perhaps it was this experience he was having in Mexico—seeing life as full of new possibilities. Perhaps he was enamored by the notion that for once he wouldn't have to be someone else's employee. When the director offered to sell him the school, Daniel saw it as an opportunity.

Through his mind whirled glorious ideas, which he enthusiastically shared with Anna over breakfast and dinner. Seeing the energy in his eyes, she couldn't help but share his vision. The school would grow to become one of the prestigious ones of the city. He'd bring his son from Indiana, who now had a college degree in education, and Anna would be a part of it all too.

What little money they had, even money borrowed on insurance policies, they put into the school. While Anna was able to bring in some extra income (she'd quit at the school for girls and found a part-time job as an English instructor for flight attendants), Daniel handled two jobs, one teaching afternoons at his own school, the other teaching mornings at another. Evenings he worked until midnight.

After several months he began to notice that in spite of his efforts to bring stability, the school was still losing students. Asking around, he learned what no one had wanted to tell him: that the teacher covering his class in the morning wasn't coming to work regularly. He began to see that undoing the harm already done in terms of reputation and educational quality was a far bigger task than he'd anticipated. He had accumulated a large debt and there was no way to repay the insurance policies.

In the beginning he'd shared his dreams for the school with Anna. Now that it was failing, he discussed none of the problems. He worked until two or three o'clock in the morning on finances, administration, class preparation. His schedule left the couple little time to talk. When he did give Anna clues about what was happening at the school, his remarks were terse. Painful as his distancing was, she recognized his unwillingness to admit his failure to the one whose confidence and support meant the most to him. In the meantime, stories of her father's business failures and the family's humiliation lurked in the back of her mind.

Her response to his withdrawal was to retreat in self-protection. She began to put all her energy, when she wasn't teaching, into being a good mother. This supported Daniel's conviction that she no longer cared what happened to the school. Two individuals who had long practiced the art of self-preservation were again internalizing their hurts and frustrations, mulling alone over the situations in which they found themselves.

Meanwhile, Daniel convinced himself that she didn't appreciate the long hours he put in trying to rescue the project. This certainty, plus his awareness that the school was going under, left him constantly depressed. And angry. When he couldn't sustain the internal agitation any longer, without any warning, he'd explode, usually at Anna.

Anna: "As long as I've known him he's had this rage, but I'd always been able to break through it, like when I used to tease, 'Growl at me, Daniel.' We both remember those times now, but it's been years since I've been able to turn his anger into laughter. The anger that developed after we moved to Mexico was different from what I had seen before. He became irrational, and if I tried to reason with him he'd become even more furious. I'd feel helpless. Everything I said was wrong. I'd try to talk about what was happening but he'd impatiently say, 'Forget it; forget it.' I couldn't get through to him.

"I don't know why, but during those years I began to take his irritation personally. He didn't come out of his anger as easily, and I couldn't be playful like I once had been. I learned that trying to discuss it wasn't the right approach, so I got to where I'd just keep quiet. If I'd understood what was going on, our relationship would have been different."

Daniel: "No, our problems were mainly my fault. Anna, or anyone else for that matter, can say something that triggers my wrath. She usually doesn't mean anything by it, but her remark will resurrect an old hurt, an old anger, and I'll get mad. She'll say, 'Daniel, I didn't mean anything by that,' but that won't stop me. She's said that I personalize too much of what people say. But for forty-nine years of my life I experienced racial discrimination. People pushed me out of the mainstream of American society, made me an outsider, and I was angry. Some of that anger is not only the result of what I experienced, but also what my grandparents and great-grandparents experienced. So I'm hyperaware of how people react to me.

"It's like when a person has a rough day at work and can't tell off the boss. The person has had to struggle to cope with things and keep his temper under control. Then when he comes home he explodes at the family over what to them seems like nothing. Naturally, the person under fire isn't going to understand what he or she did to cause such ire. I'm like that, except my day at work was forty-nine years in the United States. My fury is justified, but it's come late and is directed at the wrong people. It would be better if I could accept whatever is said and not do anything about it. But I can't do that.

"Anna speaks of justified and unjustified anger. But how can one person determine what another should or should not get angry about? If someone innocently says something that triggers a seventy-year-old hurt, who can say my wrath is unjustified?

"My anger has worked *for* me in a way though. It gave me drive. Although I'm embittered by the way American society blocked me from achieving my potential, most of my accomplishments are a result of my rage. Nobody is going to tell me I can't get an education. Nobody is going to tell me I can't work for a living in an honorable vocation. Nobody is going to run over me. So the anger gave me the drive to accomplish things.

"But it's jeopardized my relationships. I don't think I could have lived with another type of woman for forty years. When I'm angry, she doesn't come back at me. Maybe she knows that to flash back would make things worse. She's not passive, though;

she'll stand up for herself. Anna has done more for me than she's realized. She doesn't realize it because she's always wishing she'd done things differently. I know what a problem I am. She has an extraordinary personality and a good mind too. She has the ability to understand me, to know what she has to do, and to do it. I marvel at how she's been able to cope. She's a very strong person."

Anna: "I used to think I didn't get mad. I remember my father as an angry man—all the fights he and my step-mother had—and I thought I wasn't like that. I realize now that we all get angry, but I've always kept my anger inside. As a little girl I was the youngest sister, whom everyone took care of. But there were several years in there, between my mother's death and when I went to live with Violet and George, when I wasn't really taken care of. In my step-family no one tried to make me feel good. No one tried to include me, but I didn't lash out. I just went my own little way. I guess I was the only one I could talk to about my feelings, so I kept my anger inside.

"That may be one reason why it's been so hard for me to accept Daniel's rage. I understand his wrath is legitimate and that it's given him a lot of motivation to act. But I have a right to be angry too, and I don't go around making everyone miserable because of that."

WHEN HE MET Sergio, Amelio, and Mario outside the racetrack, Daniel had twenty pesos in his pocket, of which one and a half paid for his entrance. Early in the afternoon came a *quiniela*, a race in which the person placing the bet selects two horses to come in first and second, in either order. Until his voice was rasping, Daniel urged on numbers seven and nine, the horses he'd placed a bet on. They brought him winnings of seven hundred pesos.

When it was time for another *quiniela*, and he told his friends he was going to choose seven and nine again, they laughingly assured him those horses weren't going to repeat their performance. But to their amazement, to his as well, seven and nine came over the finish line ahead of all the other horses.

Altogether he had won more than two thousand pesos, a large sum of money in those times.

Saying goodbye to his friends shortly before the last race, he left to catch a bus home. He noticed there were only a few people on the bus, but with his mind reliving the day's success and contemplating the relief the winnings would bring to the family budget, he paid no attention to his fellow passengers.

When he prepared to get off at Mississippi and Avenida Reforma, two blocks from home, three other people—a woman and two men—moved to the back of the bus, as though to get off too. The woman stood to one side of him, one of the men put his hand across the door, and the other man went behind Daniel. The man whose arm blocked Daniel's exit asked, "Do you want to get off here?"

"Si."

"*Perdon,* pardon me." He moved aside and Daniel stepped from the bus, assuming the others were getting off at the next stop.

As usual, Avenida Reforma was busy and it was difficult to find a break in the traffic. Finally stepping from the curb, he started across, reaching into his pocket as he began to walk rapidly. The realization was almost enough to halt his steps in the middle of the thoroughfare. His wallet was gone. Once on the other side, he searched all his pockets, thinking maybe he'd put his wallet somewhere else. Nothing.

A stone bench along the street seemed to have been placed there for just that moment. Head in his hands, he sat on the bench and contemplated an anthill near his feet. Weighed down by crumbs, grains, and invisible burdens, they worked without stopping. From his vantage point they scurried endlessly, and for what? After all that effort, how many of them realized at the end of the day that they had accomplished absolutely nothing? "Dumb ants," he muttered aloud as he kicked the hill.

He'd gone to the races with twenty pesos and headed home with two thousand. Now he had nothing—less than he'd started out with.

Friends told him that through their mannerisms people who win at the tracks advertise where they've put the money. On the bus he'd probably often put his hand to the pocket, to be sure the money was safe there. No doubt the woman and the man who blocked his exit from the bus distracted him while the other man took the two thousand pesos.

In spite of losing the large sum but urged on by the fact that he had been able to win big once, Daniel kept going to the tracks.

Daniel: "I regret it now but I didn't even spend my weekends with Anna and the girls. I spent my Saturdays and Sundays at the racetrack. My excuse was that we needed extra money. I was always going to hit it big, then everything would become easier for us. Now I know you don't win at a racetrack, nobody beats the odds, but I had this idea that I would be the exception. Week after week, month after month, I went every Saturday and Sunday. When races started at two-thirty in the afternoon, I was there. When they ended at seven that evening, I was there. I missed the boat. I wasn't with Anna and I wasn't with the girls."

THERE WAS A strong urge to jar him awake, to say, "You belong with your family on Sundays. Your daughters need you." But she knew his reasoning could not be cracked. It was all for the family, he maintained. Well, if it was for the family, why did the family feel deprived?

When he'd kept this kind of busy schedule in the union days, she'd never wavered in her support. She'd been happy being a mother to their two beautiful daughters, especially happy knowing his involvement brought him recognition and appreciation.

But now her responsibilities at home were in addition to a job, and while she wished to adjust to this foreign land and way of life without leaning on him, she simply couldn't. They were now in their third year here, but her Spanish still wasn't fluent. The relational and coping skills she had developed in growing up seemed to do her no good in this culture. Isolated from Mexican society, she felt alone even in her own home.

Standing there, looking down at his slumbering form, her frustration made her want to shake him awake. But she caught herself and was suddenly overcome by feelings of love and understanding. In white skin he would have been destined for greatness. In his fifties his awareness that the remaining years might be few gave him a drive surpassing the desires of much younger men to aspire and achieve.

His Sundays at the racetrack remained beyond her understanding, however. While not all of the church's teachings had made the transition into adult values, she was now witnessing the way gambling could disrupt a relationship. But then maybe her condemnation was a vestige of another time, another place. In Mexico, gambling might be evidence of *machismo,* a man's need to do manly things. By embracing the Mexican culture, was Daniel also adopting the Mexican notion of manhood? Was this another disparity she'd been adjusting to?

She resisted wakening him up. Let him sleep until it was time to go to the tracks.

Despite the tensions between the two of them; despite the drives that took him away from the family; despite her own longing to be held, not just physically but emotionally as well, life must continue. What was happening to the adults should not deprive the girls of happy family times. It was a beautiful Sunday, and the three of them could be an almost-family. The girls would be delighted to spend the day swimming.

Bouncing and tumbling their naked little bodies around the room, Carla and Helena swung their swimsuits over their head. Their mother's index finger to her lips told them not to disturb Daddy, so their mouths made the motions of squeals without any accompanying sounds. Finally, dresses covering swimsuits, towels stuffed in a bag made of woven grasses, and a picnic lunch packed in a basket, the three left for the day's outing.

IT WOULD BE pleasant if the girls would come bounding into the room and leap on the bed, Daniel thought as he took his time awakening. Then they could snuggle in close to him, and the three of them would converse for awhile. After this animated father-daughter time together, they would all go downstairs, where Anna would have breakfast waiting. A cup of coffee, a glass of freshly squeezed orange juice, and a bowl of oatmeal, and he'd be ready to take the family to the park for the day. For two days he'd been planning to forego his usual trip to the tracks for some time with Anna and the girls.

He glanced over at the clock. Eleven already. They were all probably anxious for him to get up. Strange, the house was quiet. Likely they were being careful not to disturb him. Still, you'd think there would be a few sounds of activity. He sat up and tried to pick up some indication of the family's presence, but except for the tick of the clock beside the bed and the usual noises from the street below, everything was still. Slowly, he turned, put his feet on the cool floor, got up, and stretched.

Maybe they were all reading. Wait until he told them he was taking his little harem out for the day. Maybe they'd even go to the cinema after they'd played in the park and spent time at the zoo. He put on his robe and descended the stairs. At the foot of the stairs he saw the empty living room. A turn of the head told him no one was in the kitchen or dining room either.

"Anna, girls, where are you?"

His words fell flat on the floor.

"Anna. Anna," he said once more, his voice taking on a demanding tone. "Humph. You go to the trouble of staying home and planning something for your family, and what do they do? Take off without so much as a goodbye."

Going into the kitchen to get a cup of coffee, he found none. Maybe they'd be back soon, he decided as he made a pot full. Well, as soon as they got home, he'd take them to the park.

He'd forgotten how well a newspaper and a cup of coffee went together on a relaxing Sunday morning. But the luxury of that rediscovery was soon lost in a restlessness to get on with the day. If they didn't return home soon, there'd not be enough time to do all the things he'd planned. Where would they have gone? If Anna had taken the girls to church, which he doubted, they'd be home by now.

He paced the floor between the kitchen and the front window. He called Anna's friends. No, she wasn't visiting, each said. Several times he sat in the rocker by the window and tried to read the recent issue of *Time Magazine,* but powers of concentration eluded him. He went upstairs and looked in the girls' room to see if there were any clues as to where they might have gone.

Apparently Anna didn't consider the possibility of spending the day with him worth waiting around for. Whatever her plans, they included depriving him of his daughters' presence. Hours passed. Anger over being deserted ate at him as he alternately paced and read.

The happy noises of the girls preceded their appearance in the doorway. Clearly surprised at having him meet them at the door, Anna asked, "Is something the matter?"

"Yes, something's the matter. Where have you been all day?" His tone was accusing.

"Why I took the girls swimming. Is there anything wrong with that?" Her tone was defensive.

"Yes, I planned to take the family to the park and then to the cinema. And when I got up, you had already left for the day." He paused. "And without telling me where you were going." His tone was angry.

"I haven't noticed your being interested in what we've done on other Sundays." Her tone was aloof.

Anna: "The girls told me later that they got to where they hated weekends—because of Daniel always being at the races. Of course, I couldn't understand why he thought I wasn't supportive when he was trying to make the school go. I thought it was a tremendous opportunity. He's a teacher, he's a committed teacher, but he wasn't sharing with me any of what was happening to him. He was seldom home, and when he was, he was depressed. How could I express my support of something when he didn't tell me what was going on?

"I was working at the time, but my salary wasn't adequate to live on. I've always felt bad that I wasn't earning enough money to support the family. Being in a foreign country, we seemed to have no way to get financial backing. And the problems with our papers kept hanging over our head.

"I wish I could have faced these things and not had them affect me. But that's not the kind of person I am. I didn't go to pieces, but I couldn't be the relaxed, lovable person I'd been before. I was trying to reach out to him, but he was going off someplace else. And he always seemed to be misinterpreting things."

Daniel: "Now it seems immature to have become so absorbed in our financial situation. I wanted this move to be good for the family, and my idea of good was having plenty of money. In the early seventies I quit going to the track. Occasionally I'd take Anna and the girls, but the strong desire to go left me. Sometimes I think I'll go out, but I don't. Every now and then I read the results in the paper."

IN DEFEAT DANIEL finally closed his own school and went searching for a job. He found one, teaching at the Instituto nueva york, a private school with an excellent reputation.

"If you can't get along with *this* teacher," the director said in introducing Daniel to students, "you're going to be without one for the rest of the year."

During the previous term three different English teachers had been unable to control the class. Once a teacher looking to the back of the room saw a blood-covered hand sticking out of a locker—a rubber hand it turned out to be.

Daniel's determination not to stack one failure atop another enabled him to stand before this intractable class and accomplish what he was there to do. Faculty called him Maestro Winters; students affectionately called him El Teacher. During the twenty years he taught at the Instituto nueva york, Daniel never had a serious discipline problem. Once a student complained to the director that outside the classroom El Teacher was a congenial, friendly person, but unbending inside. His presence in the hall or courtyard always invited a group. On the last day of school each year, as mariachis played all day on the patio, Daniel was one of the few teachers who participated in the singing and dancing.

He was a favorite chaperon for school excursions. During the year each class traveled to a point of interest where the group stayed in hotels, visited historical sites, swam, and hiked. Often, when the bus stopped, Daniel would herd everyone off and lead them in the hokey pokey or some other dance. On the bus, students frequently requested that he sing for them. He should have been a nightclub performer, they always said.

Daniel introduced a basketball program, which began as an intramural activity and expanded to include a school team. On his file cabinet in the alcove stood a trophy won by the team he coached in a Mexico City tournament.

Girls in the school complained they didn't have equal sports opportunities. He helped them organize an intramural basketball team but insisted there wasn't enough time in the day to coach both the boys' and the girls' teams. The girls would have to find another coach. One day shortly before they were to begin playing, a group stood before Daniel, bearing a petition. Signed by every girl who planned to participate, the petition stated that no one would proceed with the project unless Daniel agreed to be their coach. He found someone else to work with the boys. For more than ten years he coached girls' basketball.

The amount of satisfaction that accompanied teaching was a marvel to him. Outside the classroom he taught sportsmanship and teamwork. Inside he taught English, the knowledge of which ensured better job opportunities for his students. Because of the school's excellent reputation in teaching English, it attracted children of political families. Mindful that this was a chance to influence the country's future leaders, Daniel was as committed to teaching principles of living as he was to teaching the subject. Speaking English, he led discussions on topics such as honesty, punctuality, relationships among people, and prejudice. Of course, boys in the advanced grades liked to discuss sex and always seemed to appreciate El Teacher's honesty and advice. The only two topics that could not be discussed were religion and politics. Given the diversity of religious backgrounds and the number of children from political families, there was too great a risk in hurting someone's feelings.

Friday was called Social Friday. Rather than play games, as most classes did, Daniel's groups preferred discussions. "Tell us about when you were a boy," students frequently requested. And Daniel would describe privies, how they were cleaned, childhood memories of kids daring each other to put their tongue against the outdoor pump spigot on icy cold mornings, and life before electricity.

His success could have brought new vitality into the marriage. It didn't. Anna tried to persuade him that they should see a marriage counselor, a third party to listen to them and offer insight or direction.

"If someone's depressed," he argued, "they've got to work that out inside themselves. A psychiatrist can't do any more for me than I can do for myself. You know what your problem is, what its origin is, and you know why. It's a matter of admitting to yourself, of being honest, then you can get to the basis of it. It's difficult, but I think everyone should be able to do it."

"You said people know what the origin of the problem is," she would argue back. "Sometimes we don't know, or we don't want to admit what it is."

"It seems like a weakness in an individual if you have to go to someone else to work out your problems. Besides, I read that psychiatrists in the U.S. have a high suicide rate. If they're supposedly helping you—they have greater problems than their patients."

"Well, of course, some of them have conflicts themselves. They are human, you know. Which probably makes them more able to understand other people's problems."

He'd done it again, she thought later. He'd taken something personal, a conflict between the two of them, and turned it into an abstraction. The discussion wasn't about their relationship anymore; it was about psychiatrists.

PEOPLE CRAMMED INTO a small space; drinks flowing; music, heavy on the bass, coming from a stereo system. All around Anna everyone was speaking Spanish, a rapid progression of words that passed over her like a jet streaking across the sky. A few tried to initiate a conversation, among them the principal's wife and a middle-aged woman married to one of the math teachers.

Exhausted from efforts to communicate, she took a glass of wine into a corner and sat down in a leather folding chair. On the other side of the room she watched Daniel carrying on an animated conversation with a cluster of men. Laughter erupted, over something he'd said, it appeared, evidence that his ability to make friends extended across cultures.

Weren't there any shy Mexican women?

She spent the rest of the evening, three hours altogether, in the same corner. Every now and then someone would look over and smile, but no one came to talk with her. Not that she minded; she had no energy left for conversation.

On the way home all Daniel could talk about was how much fun the party was. *A great group of colleagues* he kept saying. She understood. In all the time they'd been married, the only parties he'd been invited to were hosted by Negroes: bridge parties, an evening of men playing poker. Being among professionals, accepted as an equal—it was a new experience, and not surprisingly he was reaping the benefits of his ease in making friends.

He paused to take a breath. "You're quiet. Didn't you have a good time?"

He'd spent decades feeling isolated, separate. She could stand one evening of discomfort.

"Yes," she said, "it was fun."

But there were other parties, other evenings when Daniel was involved in conversation, the center of attention even. She, on the other hand, wasn't comfortable initiating social interaction, and even when others approached her, she was aware of how quickly they moved on, as if they'd done their duty and could now talk with someone they liked.

She didn't complain but Daniel did. "You're too reserved. You give the impression you don't like anyone. And you need to wear a smile," he advised. "Mexicans like happy people."

Anna: "I know I'm not outgoing. I have to learn to know people before I feel comfortable with them. But I'm not that way because I don't like them. I made friends, but he always found something wrong with them, said he didn't want to be a hypocrite. He never made any effort to enter into my relationships."

Daniel: "I do tend to be outgoing—that is, if I like the person. At the school where I worked most of our years here, I developed several good relationships. But those only seemed to work when I was by myself. When Anna was around—at some of the social events, people seemed to more or less clam up, like they didn't know what to do with her.

"There have been certain aspects about Anna that I wish were different. I think there was something about her religious background that has limited her ability to relate to other people. Her church had a separatist tradition. Persecution forced them to stick together. Maybe it was the persecution, maybe the fact that they spoke German while their neighbors spoke English, but for many years after the group came to the U.S., they had limited contact with people outside their own little group. I think it got to the point where they approached those outside their group in fear."

Anna: "It's like I said, when we came here, Daniel became a part of Mexico, but he never tried to help me become a part of it too."

Chapter 12

*L*YING IN BED, *Anna marvels at the way in which they have moved beyond their original story-telling intentions to a new level of healing. At first the narration was familiar to them both, episodes they've spent forty years dissecting. In the last day or two, instead of speaking to Nancy or to the recorder, they have more often directed the conversation to each other. Several times, Daniel, who usually prefers discussing facts rather than feelings has described a reaction or emotion she's never known about. Likewise, he sometimes seems startled by her words, saying, "I didn't know you felt that way." He says he wouldn't be able to talk like this in front of most people.*

Aware that his body is only inches from hers, stretched from the headboard to the bottom of the mattress, she has an urge to press hers against him. No, such an action would no doubt startle him, and she'd be left disappointed by his response.

So tomorrow they finish telling the story. Sunday they take a day off for fun together, and Monday Nancy leaves. Returns home knowing many details about their lives but lacking any information about—some would claim it is the defining event of their marriage. Not she. No, she won't accept it as anything more than getting sidetracked.

This week has offered its own kind of resurrection, *a word from her Sunday School days. Death—in this case the death of a marriage—was conquered. But how can you have a resurrection without somebody getting crucified?*

The fourteen year gap they've only hinted at. The perceptive ear would have caught the clues and asked more questions. But she knows from her own experience: we hear what we want to hear. Not that theirs isn't the story of love they've made it out to be.

Velma, who knows all about those fourteen years, says their story is evidence that love is flawed. Not flawed, Anna always argues; it's human behavior that's flawed, not love. We act according to our needs, according to our capacity and at the level of our development. Communication between Daniel and her broke down because of human error, not because they were from two races, not because love is flawed. You'll always be the optimist, Velma reminds her.

This was to be a story about a biracial marriage. Not that their being of two races has turned out to be a minor factor. Anna recognizes that although their marriage made a statement to society, their story, even in this incomplete form, turns out to be about how two people who love each other have faced both day-by-day living and crises.

It's too bad the whole story can't be told, though. After fourteen years—actually sixteen years of struggle, if you count the last two—she and Daniel have finally triumphed.

No, love has triumphed.

THEY ALL LAUGHED as Carla sat on the suitcase while Anna latched it. She was glad the girls had responded positively to being left with Hannah who, forty-eight and never married, didn't have the kind of personality that children easily warmed up to. But out of her affection for Anna she had offered to keep the girls for a week while their parents took a vacation.

Years had passed since the two of them had gone away together.

After helping the girls get settled at Hannah's, she and Daniel rushed to the parking lot where the tour group was to meet. She wore a turquoise cotton sundress with a short jacket in a floral print, he a yellow guayabera shirt, both outfits suitable for Cancun. As they waited to board the bus, the tour director moved among the passengers, all of them teachers from schools in Mexico City, trying to make everyone feel welcome. He was a good-natured man with bushy black hair and a wide smile, who considered their enjoyment of the trip his responsibility.

Once they boarded, Daniel, stretching his long legs into the aisle, leaned toward Anna and told her she mustn't worry about the girls. She had no intention of worrying. She rested her hand on his leg and told him he mustn't think about school all week. He had no intention of thinking about school.

The bus had barely left Mexico City when the tour director stood and began speaking through a microphone.

"Since we're going to spend a week in each other's company, wouldn't you like to know who your travel companions are?"

"Sí," the passengers responded in unison.

Like a talk show host, he carried a microphone down the aisle, asking everyone to tell something about themselves. He responded in a manner that invited each traveler to become part of the fun.

"My name is Anna Winters," she said when the microphone was thrust in front of her face.

"I detect an American accent, Anna. How long have you been in Mexico?"

"Six years."

"You're probably the only one on this bus who's going to have to be careful not to get a sunburn." He turned away from her to make eye contact up and down the aisle. "Now I want to remind you that we're going to have to look out for each other this week. That means it's everyone's responsibility to keep Anna from getting a sunburn. Do you understand? If you see her turning a little pink, you are to take off your shirt—that includes you ladies—and cover her. If you must"—he now spoke in a dramatic tone accompanied by large sweeping gestures—"pick her up and carry her out of the sunshine."

The group laughed. "And what about you, sir? Are you also from the United States?"

"I was born there, but I'm as Mexican..." Daniel paused for dramatic effect. "I'm as Mexican as *chile verde.*" The other passengers cheered. For the rest of the journey, whenever they wanted to stretch, members of the group would stand in the aisle beside Daniel, chatting amiably.

Barely had the vacationers had time to go to their rooms and freshen up before they were expected at a party in one of the hotel's large conference rooms. Mariachis played; drinks flowed. When everyone had had time to get into the spirit of the evening, the director gathered the group around him.

"What we need is a king and queen, someone to rule over us, someone with royalty in their blood." The tour group elected beautiful twenty-two year old Lorita as its queen; Daniel was crowned King Chile Verde Primero.

By the end of the evening Anna already knew the vacation was a mistake. If the first day was any indication, this was going to be a week-long party with King Chile Verde Primero and a twenty-two year old woman the centers of attention.

Anna: "I understood that in Latin America marriages like ours, two people of different races or ethnic groups, were accepted, so I expected everything to work out easily down here.

"But this feeling that Daniel had—finally feeling free—I didn't have. I'd always been free. In the United States I was part of the privileged group. Here I was the outsider, the foreigner. And I had no background in Spanish, a fact that has remained a barrier. People still ask me why I don't speak better after all these years, and if someone meets both of us at the same time, they'll often ask why his Spanish is so much better than mine.

"I strongly agreed with our reason for moving to Mexico. I could verbally express my understanding of how Daniel felt, but the fact that the move was not the freeing experience for me that it was for him created problems for us.

"I began to be upset by superficial things—the many problems we had with getting our papers, the economic uncertainty we lived with for so long. Daniel didn't understand why I didn't feel this wonderful sense of freedom he was experiencing. He didn't understand why I saw these other things as so important. For example, when I was upset about our car being confiscated, he shrugged and said that having lived as a colored man in the United States, he'd had far worse things happen to him.

"I don't know if it was my maternal instincts, or what. Maybe at times I became preoccupied with the girls' needs and ignored his. I kept telling myself that the move was good for them; it was good for our marriage; that if we'd stayed in Richmond, we never would have been a part of the community anyway. But here we were in Mexico City, and the special relationship we had as a family no longer existed.

"In those first years, when he was experiencing the exhilaration of being free, I was feeling abandoned. Everyone who knows him knows he's an American by birth but that his soul is Mexican."

Daniel: "During those years we each knew we were growing apart, but something kept holding us together. And it wasn't something that only the two of us recognized. Several times I've sat down with the girls and they've talked frankly about our family. They've never been judgmental toward me or their mother, but they've told Anna at times they don't know why she put up with so much. Through everything we haven't lost our relationship. We have a wonderful family.

"Many people with fewer problems than we had have separated or divorced. In spite of everything Anna and I haven't. Now we don't feel so far apart. I feel close to her, and I know she feels close to me. When you feel closeness like this, you both know it.

"I never forget that Anna gave up everything to marry me, that being married to me has deprived her of many opportunities. If she'd married a white man, she would still have close family ties; she would have the career she wanted; she would have her country.

"Anna is very, very idealistic. She thinks things should never change, that there's no reason for change. Love should keep that bloom that it's always had. I think it may be basically there, but that it's like a flower that blooms in seasons. It isn't always a beautiful blossom, but the basic plant is there. Other things in life, such as responsibilities, interfere, change the flower to some extent, take away its beauty for awhile. It can't always be the beautiful flower that you can hold up as an ideal."

Anna: "Yes, I am idealistic. But Daniel's wrong; I know relationships change, people change. Life doesn't stay the same. I felt that what had existed between us was still there. I knew it.

"When Daniel and I married I thought I was the luckiest woman in the world. I was sure no one had ever been in love the way we were. Infatuation is not the opposite of love; infatuation is a part of love. Infatuation is the joy of discovery, excitement that something new has entered your life. Newly discovered love makes you idealistic, and the recognition you give each other is very affirming. I thought Daniel had tremendous potential; he thought I was sensitive and intelligent. We would create this wonderful life together.

"I never allowed myself to see the problems that already existed. Perhaps ours being a biracial marriage kept me from seeing them. My friends raised concerns about how society's view of our marriage would affect our relationship and about the problems our children would face. I was sure we could handle those problems, so I was taken by surprise when these other problems emerged, the ordinary ones that can separate people. I was so sure I wouldn't get lost in the forest that I hadn't paused to wonder if there were any bear traps. We brought to the relationship our differing temperaments, our individual likes and dislikes, disturbing habits. And these were no small differences. I knew that in marriage it was not only futile but damaging to try to change someone, yet I had no idea what I should do. Should I simply endure the problems?

"A fallacy in my thinking was the belief that the two of us could handle life. But a relationship isn't just two people. There's a world out there, external factors that have had a profound affect on us. I don't mean just the social structure and the repercussions of racism. I mean the everyday encounters—the job, the friends, the business encounters.

"Yet during those years in Minnesota and Indiana there were enough times of renewal to keep our love alive. Learning to live with a person, even someone you deeply love, is a difficult adjustment to make. I would say couples need those renewal times. It's like recharging your battery.

"After our move here those times of renewal became less frequent, then nonexistent. The recognition and affirmation that had been so important in our relationship turned unto a cycle of letting each other down. Those are two important words for me—*recognition* and *affirmation*. We experience affirmation when someone recognizes what we have to offer. We blossom when we get recognition; we wither when we don't get it. I began to feel he was no longer giving me the recognition I needed. That void affected me so that I couldn't give him what he needed either, and he became angry that I wasn't able to be the way I'd been before.

"Daniel can be very charming when he wants to be. So he was able to evoke a positive response from the people he came in daily contact with. If I couldn't give him the recognition he needed, he'd go somewhere else. But for me, someone who's unable to be outgoing and charming, it was difficult getting the recognition and affirmation I needed.

"Then he began to do things that made me think, *This isn't really Daniel.* He would get to reacting in this negative way, and I was trying to explain, trying to help him understand. He would react to something someone said, or something I said in a completely emotional way, and there was no way I could tune into that, no way I could make him look at things rationally. He would say I was against him, which wasn't true at all. I wondered what in the world is going on here? How can he think that?

"Over time—after familiarity, parenting, financial pressures, and everyday decision-making became a part of the relationship—the intoxicating infatuation had worn away. But I believe that what is real, stays. That soul-deep bond, the oneness that has been created from two lives, remains.

"In 1981 we drove back to Indiana and brought back some of the things we had stored there. I had all of the letters Daniel had written. Reading them reinforced my conviction that the distance between us couldn't be true. What he said and the way he treated me, the poems he wrote elicited from me such a deep response of love. He put into writing the feelings that were inside me too. Each of us responded to the other in a way that kept our love growing and growing. When I showed him one of the letters his response wasn't *I want to reread that.* His reaction was, *That was another time.*

"I was idealistic because our relationship had been a spiritual one. It had reached inside me, into my very spirit. I got through those later difficult times because I just couldn't believe our spiritual connectedness could go away. At the same time I couldn't understand why—knowing he had felt that same spiritual bond—we were having such a difficult time coming together now.

"In our years together he had shown me a part of himself that few people knew. Now it was so painful to acknowledge to myself that I was only getting the same glimpses everyone else got."

Chapter 13

EVERY TIME ANNA looks in Daniel's direction, he appears light-hearted. He's actually humming a tune as he squeezes the orange juice. She stirs the oatmeal with more deliberate strokes, her steps toward the dining room slower. She stands behind the chair, hesitant, unsure of whether she wants to sit and enter the breakfast conversation.

Surprisingly he was the one to suggest they talk about it. In bed last night, leaning on his elbow and facing her he said, "We've opened up with each other and with her. It doesn't seem right not to tell her everything." Anna resisted the notion, not because she disagreed with his intent, but because the pain has long been stored in remote caverns. Sealed off, too, she's believed, until the conversations of recent days stuck a wedge deep into her heart. She's not sure she'll be able to handle the crushing weight of the full story.

But it makes little sense to tell about the history of their love then omit an important detail. A very important detail. Besides, she's been committed to truth her whole life. Now hardly seems the time to back away.

Will Nancy understand the degree of strength it takes to live with someone who's betrayed you? Will she understand the determination required for a woman to hold on to love?

Now, at the breakfast table they drink the fresh orange juice and eat the oatmeal sprinkled with brown sugar. Anna sits silently, suddenly reminded by her fingernails digging into the palm of her hand of how tightly she's holding the spoon. Daniel doesn't say much either, until he pushes his chair away from the table, crosses his long legs, and clasps the top knee with both hands.

"What do O'Henry's stories have in common?" he asks Nancy.

Nancy hesitates, surely wondering about the origins of this question. "Well, I guess you could say their characters are usually down and out."

"What else?" Anna isn't sure where he's going either.

"Well—uh—uh."

"They have surprise endings. Tonight we're going to give you the surprise ending for your book."

As they go through the day they've planned, Anna dreads each activity as if it's a corner they will go around only to discover a monster, a calamity. At the Christian Science church (a surprise in itself that Daniel would suggest the three of them go) she prays for strength. From church they go to a German restaurant for lunch, then sightseeing.

When they've finished an evening snack, washed and put away the dishes, Daniel leads the way into the living room. Her stomach filled with knots, her whole body feeling the weight of what is about to come, she takes her usual seat at the end of the sofa. As if she's looking through the large end of binoculars, she watches Daniel walk over to the mantle and remove the picture that is always there.

"This," he says, "is my twelve-year-old son, Terrell."

ANNA COULDN'T DENY the distance that had come between them. At the end of the day, when they returned home from their separate jobs, after she'd asked *How was your day?* and he'd said *Fine,* they either ate dinner in silence or discussed impersonal topics, such as the weather or politics. Every now and then she urged him to communicate more. *When I have something to say, I'll say it,* he'd grunt.

He made no effort to hide from her the fact that he was going to a party or a dinner with friends, and that she wasn't welcome. He'd long been blunt about the *why*: her reserve that came across as aloofness, snobbery. Seated alone at the table, the radio tuned to the news, she'd eat leftovers, trying to convince herself that she'd just as soon stay home; she was as uncomfortable with his friends as they were with her.

When did this sense that all was not right in their marriage change to one of suspicion? First the telephone calls: Estela calling about school business, Daniel said. But she could tell his tone on the phone was guarded. She knew who Estela was: the school secretary—why, she couldn't be thirty yet. At sixty-three he was too old for such a young woman, Anna told herself. That was before she read in the news that an older celebrity had fathered the child of a young film star. Besides, she as well as anyone knew how enchanting Daniel could be.

Then the letters. She was looking for stamps in the center desk drawer when she came upon something else: two letters from Japan, addressed to Daniel. She knew Estela was vacationing in Japan, but you send postcards when you make such a trip, she thought. Unless you have more to say. Unless there's a special relationship. Briefly she was tempted to look inside the envelopes. No, she'd never been that kind of wife, and she wasn't going to begin snooping now. She would come right out and ask him.

As soon as he stepped from the front door into the foyer, before he even had time to loosen his tie and hang up his jacket, she planted her body in front of his. "I found the letters," she said, waving them in the air. Her tone was more hostile than she intended.

Immediately Daniel went on the offensive, accusing her of reading his private mail. His accusation seemed to confirm her uneasiness; otherwise, why would it matter?

"You don't have to lie. It's worse when you lie to me."

She regretted not waiting until sometime later in the evening when they were both seated. Standing in the foyer forced her to look up at him. And he was using their difference in height to full advantage: pulling back his shoulders, thrusting his chest forward as if daring her to throw a punch. Which was what she wanted to do: pound him. Pound him with all her might. Instead, she targeted her hazel eyes on his dark ones, which glared back in defiance.

But she knew him well enough to recognize that he was also relieved. Daniel, who'd long insisted he couldn't be a hypocrite when it came to being nice to her friends, couldn't stand being one in his marriage either, it seemed.

"You're right," he said. But instead of appearing ashamed or sorry, he went on the attack. "You think just because we've been married a long time—you take me for granted. A man needs affirmation, Anna, a fact you seem to have forgotten. And affection. Estela gives me both. If you hadn't changed..."

That night she slept in the guest room. Rather, she tried to sleep. Curled up, hugging her knees, she nursed her pain. As a young child she'd lost her mother; her father had taken off out West without even saying goodbye. But no hurt could match the feeling of abandonment she felt that night and during the many nights that followed.

SHE'D BEEN THINKING about how she might win Daniel back. The man wanted affirmation and affection. When better to offer both than in time of illness, while he was home with salmonella? She left work early, stopping by the market down the street for fresh flowers.

"Hi, I'm home," she called in false cheerfulness from the foyer a fraction of a second before spotting Estela descending the staircase.

She had tried to convince herself that Daniel's little speech about his needs fully explained his attraction. But as Estela came downstairs, her flared skirt and wide-necked cotton blouse gave her a fluidity of movement. Her perky breasts and smooth complexion represented youthfulness and vitality. Anna pushed from her mind the image of Daniel running his fingers through the dark hair resting on her competitor's shoulders.

She saw herself as she surely appeared in the younger woman's eyes: hair with streaks of gray mixed with the blond, facial lines that like cracks in the earth witnessed to weather's vicissitudes, lightly sagging jowls, breasts that sagged too.

"It appears we have something in common," she said sarcastically as Estela, eyes downcast, walked past her and wordlessly opened the door.

After dumping the flowers in the trash can, Anna went upstairs to the bedroom she and Daniel no longer shared and announced, "I will not have that woman in my house."

Later she would berate herself for confronting him and Estela. If she'd ignored his behavior, she came to believe, he would have become bored and ended the other relationship. Instead it seemed to become a battle of wills. He was a man and would not let a woman tell him what to do or not do.

Then came nights when he didn't even call to tell her he wouldn't be home. Lonely nights when she lay awake until dawn, her heart pushing against her ribs with so much force she cried out in pain. Only the walls heard.

After hurt came anger. Here they were approaching the later years of their life, a time when couples who loved each other might find peace and pleasure just being together. Her mothering responsibilities were over and she was ready to give some of her own wishes priority. One of those wishes was to spend time enjoying the company of the man she loved. Now he was throwing it all away, her life as well as his own.

After anger a sense of utter helplessness.

SEVERAL TIMES SHE warned Daniel to be careful, to take precautions against getting the woman pregnant. His response was short, impatient: he could handle things.

Then came the announcement: "Estela is pregnant." Grief stacked atop grief: for the unwed mother, for this child to be brought into such a crazy situation, for herself. It was a son, Terrell, named after Daniel's childhood friend.

With the boy's birth, Daniel began to spend more time at Estela's, often an entire weekend. The boy needed a father, he argued.

"If you enjoy her company so much," Anna said, "go live there. I can get along by myself."

Yet she knew—and Daniel too, most likely—that was not true. Her options were limited. She was nearly sixty, teaching English to flight attendants and engineers, not making nearly enough money to live on. Briefly she considered moving back to the States, where she had friends and could support herself. But she'd been out of the social work field too long to resume that career, and friends, she knew, would have changed. She'd been away twenty years, too long to return to anything resembling what she'd left behind. Besides, Carla and Helena had both married Mexicans. Mexico was their home.

Sometimes she preferred being alone. At other times she wanted his presence, painful as it was to look at him and know he now lacked commitment to their marriage. Then when he *was* with her, she could only verbally attack him.

Daniel: "Things reached a point where it seemed Anna and I were no longer compatible. We had a lot of arguments."

Anna: "She didn't argue with you, and I was supposed to be the same way. I don't know how we managed to live together those thirteen years, but we did. The whole time, though, there were emotional ups and downs, hope one day, despair the next. I'd think, we've got this problem licked, then he'd disappear for the weekend. Sometimes things became so intense that I told him to go away. If we couldn't have the quality of relationship I needed and he needed, then I preferred not having any relationship at all."

Daniel: "But if you love a person and there's a union that exists, how can you say, 'I can get along without you' and at the same time say, 'How much I love you'?"

Anna: "That's something you'll never understand. I just said I didn't want to have a relationship that didn't have the qualities we both needed. If the qualities aren't there for the relationship that we once had and that I know is good for both of us, then we shouldn't be together. I don't know why you can't understand that."

Daniel: "I don't think you should even bring that up: 'I love him but I can't live with him.' That's a fallacy. It can't be true."

Anna: "What I mean is that if people really love, they're going to try to do something about it. Relationships are give and take. I just didn't think the relationship we had established could be destroyed."

In 1979, when Terrell turned five, Daniel decided to go live with him and Estela. For Anna it was a familiar sorrow, one that ran deep and scraped the marrow of her being. It resurrected a distinct childhood memory of being the only one without a real family, the only one without the love of a mother and father.

Daniel: "I felt this: My children in the States were married. Carla and Helena were grown. Here was this little fellow growing up. He needed my support as a father."

But after eight months Daniel decided he didn't want to live with Estela any longer and came back to Anna. Still, he didn't give up the other relationship; he continued to spend some nights and weekends with Estela and Terrell. When he was home with Anna they had bitter arguments.

Daniel: "Of course Anna, being my wife, had a right to be angry. I understood. I knew I was in the wrong, but in those kinds of circumstances you automatically try to defend yourself. I felt guilty about it, to the point that to escape the fights, to escape the truth Anna was telling me, I'd go back out to Estela's. There everything was always peaceful.

"Estela's Mexican, and she's more dependent. It's part of the culture here; the man is treated like a king. So she would do things that Anna wouldn't do. Like she wouldn't let me wash a dish. That's not a man's job. Anna's too independent. I'm not criticizing her for it. For many years Anna treated me like a king, too, but then it disappeared. A woman can treat a man like a king and still be independent. Treating him like a king doesn't mean being his slave; it's showing him consideration."

Anna: "He used to make me feel the same way, like a queen. It wasn't that he was coddling me; he was making me feel special."

THE GENTLE CRACKLE of the fire, the clink of teacups against saucers. An intimate setting. One Anna would have liked to have shared with Daniel. Not that she wasn't glad for her friend Evelyn's companionship, but her heart ached for his presence.

Just as the flames consumed the wood she'd stacked in the fireplace—to ward off the cool of an October evening as much as provide ambiance—Anna felt herself being consumed. She recalled the independent young woman who had set out for Chicago following her junior year of college. The idealistic young woman who'd taken the train to New York right after graduation. Only a few days after learning to drive she'd gone to northern Indiana, determined to make a difference in the world. The woman she once was, adventurous and independent, now on the verge of extinction.

"What?" Evelyn asked. Apparently Anna had expressed that last thought half aloud.

"The woman I once was is on the verge of extinction."

"I've said it before, that man's destroying you. Sucked up all your energy, and now he's spitting you out."

"I don't know—it's completely out of character."

"How can you keep saying that? He's been with this woman, how many years now? It's not like this is some short fling. You've got to quit letting him come and go at will."

"I can't."

"But all of this back-and-forth, back-and-forth business is turning you into an angry, bitter woman."

"I know. I know."

From the sidewalk, no further than three feet from the living room window, came the shouts of young people. An object made a thump against the pane. Followed by laughter.

"If I'd just put more effort into studying Spanish," Anna said. "Made a better adjustment to Mexico…"

"You're still blaming yourself? Stop it. The man's a—" Evelyn stopped abruptly, as if monitoring her thoughts.

"No, whatever you were going to say, he's not. Something's just come over him. If I'm patient he'll realize his mistake and come home to stay."

Evelyn reached across the chasm between their chairs, too far to actually touch, but it was a symbolic action, her tone sympathetic. "I know you want to believe that."

"It's true. I know him better than anyone. Besides, she's young. She'll get tired of—"

"You can't just wait for him to come around. You've got to take care of yourself."

"I am. I invited you over for supper, didn't I? That's taking care of myself."

Evelyn's response to that was a *humph*.

"More tea?" Anna asked, reaching for the teapot on the small round table beside her. Evelyn held out her cup. A loud pop from the fireplace startled both women. The empty teacup rattled in its saucer.

"Just look at what he's doing to you, raising your spirits the minute he comes in that door, sending them plummeting the next."

"I've seen plenty of marriages. Most don't come near approximating the relationship Daniel and I had. Not in terms of passion or friendship. I can't let all that go."

"Well, he certainly seems ready to. Has already. Just let the man leave. Whatever happens, happens. Let him take the consequences."

"I can't do that."

"So you think that one of these days he's going to come to his senses and the two of you will be able to pick up where you left off?"

"Well, not quite in the same place. But yes, I picture us spending the rest of our years walking and talking and laughing and loving. If I decided to close the door on our marriage…"

"Anna, it's not like you to be a doormat. I've always thought of you as a strong woman. But here you are, letting this man—"

"He's not just *this* man. He's the man I love. I know myself, I know Daniel, and I know our former relationship better than anybody else. Besides, my decisions have never been based on what people think. No matter what he does, I'm not going to be the one to bring the marriage to an end."

Two close friends. One trying to nudge the other back to a reality that would save her from continued heartache, the other entrenched in defiance and denial.

Anna: "Am I a doormat? We live in a society that categorizes people. If you don't stand up for what you want, you're a doormat. No one could understand that I still believed in the Daniel I knew, and in our marriage."

She decided finally that she would continue to let him come and go. However, she would work at becoming emotionally detached. Though she loved him as much as a woman could love a man, she did not need him. She'd been abandoned as a child and discovered ways to survive the hurt. Drawing upon those same internal resources, the ability to engage yet protect herself, she again took on the physical posture that had won the Women's Athletic Association award during her college years: straight back, uplifted chin. She decided that until Daniel came back to stay, she would get along quite fine.

But her attitude perplexed him. She said she loved him yet acted aloof. Many times she calmly told him, "Go ahead, go back to Estela. I'll get along." She never begged him to stay, while Estela would get down on her knees and rest her head on his lap, pleading with him to stay with her. The only person her decision made sense to was herself.

Anna: "I didn't stay in this marriage because I thought I couldn't live alone or because of my limited financial options. I stayed because of how I felt about our relationship, about the qualities that should be kept. Even if he wasn't going to be faithful to our marriage covenant, I would be. I defied the world when I married Daniel. I defied the world again when I went through all this."

Over the years the arrangement, his living with Anna but spending long blocks of time with Estela, became ordinary. The two of them, Anna and Daniel, were not simply two people occupying the same house. In many ways life went on as it had before. They often conversed about politics, household business, what was happening in each of their lives. The romance was gone, but they still had their friendship. They even talked about their relationship. Of course, things had happened in their marriage, she told him; problems emerge in every marriage. But you either run away or you try to solve them.

For Anna, in spite of her determination to be self-contained, there were emotional ups and downs: hope one day, despair the next. She'd believe they had reestablished a commitment, then Daniel would be gone for a weekend.

Anna: "He could go off and have a pleasurable experience with her, but he couldn't do what was necessary in our relationship. I told him over and over, 'If you'd given me what you've been giving her, things would have been different for us.' But I got nothing."

Daniel: "I wasn't able to make a clean break from Anna. I knew what we'd had together; I had all these memories. After I moved to Estela's, I used to look at Anna's picture and cry. I couldn't understand what had happened.

"At times I feel for her and Estela. I've been pretty much of a heel. I've deeply hurt Anna, and I've damaged Estela's life. She's forty-two now. If I hadn't come on the scene, she might have been happily married. So I feel like I ruined two lives."

Fourteen years after their relationship began, eighteen months prior to the interview, Estela gave Daniel an ultimatum:

either he live with her or with Anna. His daughters were grown and didn't need him, but Terrell needed a father, she said, one who didn't just pop in and out of his life. Daniel knew she was right; he did have obligations to the boy. But he couldn't decide.

A conversation he'd had four years earlier, when he was seventy-two, kept coming to mind. Terrell attended the school where Estela worked and where Daniel had taught. When the boy began creating discipline problems, the school psychologist called Daniel in for a consultation. She asked him, "If you were sick, who would you rather take care of you, Estela or Anna?"

"Anna," he'd said without hesitating. The quickness of his response surprised him. He knew he could depend more on her.

Finally he and Estela agreed that if he couldn't stay with her permanently, they would separate. Yet there was not a complete break in the relationship; they continued to come together around Terrell's needs. Daniel bought his school uniforms, books, and sundry needs. When he applied for his pension for the years he had worked at International Harvester, he learned that his son could receive a small monthly check. He also continued to take Terrell to karate classes, and during soccer season went out on Saturday mornings to cheer his team on. Sometimes, when transportation problems arose, Daniel would pick him up and deliver him to his grandmother's house. The previous year Terrell had celebrated Christmas with Daniel, Anna, and their daughters' families.

With Daniel back home Anna felt no sense of victory. She'd never stopped loving him, but for fourteen years she'd felt marginal. She'd assumed the relationship with Estela would end, that Daniel would tire of it. But he never had, and she was convinced that if she'd made the same demand, *either Estela or me*, Daniel would have chosen Estela.

LATER SUNDAY EVENING, the final day of the interview, Anna's and Daniel's older daughter, Carla, came by the house with her three young children. She was a lovely woman, in her thirties, with a light brown complexion, dark wavy hair, and her father's easy smile. After the children visited with their grandparents, she took them upstairs and put them to bed, then joined the conversation.

Carla: "It's part of Mexican life. Many men are married and they have other families. In Mexico we don't call them illegitimate children; we call them *hijos naturales*, natural children. We have neighbors, where I'm sure the man has another family. He appears every fifteen days, coming at night and ringing the bell. He leaves early in the morning. There are three kids. I remember a family at school. Their father had—I don't know how many kids, all over Mexico. He had two sets of children at the school.

"We call it *la casa grande* and *la casa chica*. Many times the children of the little house know about the children of the big house, but at *la casa grande* nobody knows about *la casa chica*.

"It was a big shock at first and hard to accept. The more I thought about it the more I realized we didn't have to feel bad. I've come to look at it differently over the years."

Anna: "There are many women in Mexico who know there's another woman. They know there's another family. But there's something wrong here. We—that is women—are not being honest about what that does to us. Instant gratification—I feel that's what men seek. I can't understand why, if you have a relationship you've developed that has all these wonderful things going for it, why you wouldn't want to keep it that way. My only answer is, I'm a woman, and I wish a man would sit down and explain it to me."

Daniel: "So our story has a happy ending. I don't know what would have happened if Anna had been another type of woman. My life might have been a disaster. But as it is, we've picked up the pieces and I think we're beginning to find ourselves, returning to what we once had. I think Anna feels more stable and more secure and more tranquil with our relationship than she has for a long time. This is just my opinion. I won't say that she's completely trusting; she is on her guard to a certain extent. She's hoping things will continue as they are and that nothing will interfere. But she's not sure. I may be wrong, but I think that's how she feels."

Anna: "I don't even think of that. I accept the situation as it is at the moment. I don't doubt his love. I never did. He never said he didn't love me anymore. One of the painful realizations, though, is that he could have found other women who responded, many of them. So I'm in the same category. I'm just one of the women who's responded.

"In terms of our current relationship, we're going in the right direction. What we've been doing has been great. But I don't think Daniel understands—the thing I want is impossible. I want it all never to have happened. I give him credit for trying to make up for lost time. In many ways he's been wonderful, and I appreciate that, but they feel like lost years.

"Before we married I saw couples whose lives seemed so prosaic, and I was determined not to have that kind of marriage. To have a dull marriage is even worse than what we've been through. When difficulties arise in an unexciting marriage, there's nothing better to develop, nothing to look back on. I don't mean this to be trite, but I think we learn from things that go wrong. We learn from suffering. If we don't, what's life all about?

"We've been talking about love, but love is tied up with the whole business of living. Maybe I'm being overly idealistic, but I think learning to live is working things out and going on from there. And as we stumble along, we probably can only learn for ourselves. We can't pass our wisdom on to our children; they have to learn from their own experiences. As parents we can only prepare them to face up to whatever comes along. These things happen generation after generation.

"What have I learned? That what I've always believed was right: If you have something of value, you don't run away. You try to keep it and learn how to live creatively with the tension that's come about. I have this idea that when we're confronted by negative realities, we must continue working for harmony in our own life. We must keep trying to understand ourselves and our relationships."

DANIEL DIED FIVE months after our time together. Over the years Inez and Anna had kept in touch through Christmas cards. In 1989 their college class celebrated its fiftieth reunion. Inez and a college friend who had done well financially sent Anna money for plane fare. When Inez met her at the Indianapolis airport, she was struck by how thin and pale Anna was. She wasn't talkative and left Inez quite unsatisfied with their time together. Anna only attended the banquet, then traveled to northern Indiana to visit her cousins.

Inez assumed Anna looked bad because she was facing a lonely life. However, Anna died of cancer a short time later.

"I see her life as bittersweet," Inez wrote. "Bitter in unfulfilled childhood needs and unfaithful love, sweet in Anna's reaching out beyond her abandonment as a child. As her friend, I hope that *forever* will bring fully to her what this life denied."

ENDNOTES

[1] Kathleen M. Blee, *Women of the Klan: Racism and Gender in the 1920s* (Berkeley: University of California Press, 1991), 109.

[2] Ida Wells, in her autobiography put the count at 150; however, Elliot Rudwick's *Race Riot in East St. Louis* estimates the number to be closer to thirty-nine.

[3] Wells, Ida B., *Crusade for Justice: the Autobiography of Ida B. Wells* (Chicago: The University of Chicago Press, 1970), 391. See also Rudwick, Elliot, *Riot in East St. Louis, July 2, 1917* (Carbondale: Southern Illinois Press, 1964).

[4] Except for this, all the letters in the book were in Anna's or Violet's possession. I composed this one based on Anna's memory.

[5] For a helpful and interesting interpretation of romantic comedy of the thirties, read Elizabeth Kendall, *The Runaway Bride* (New York: Knopf, 1990).

[6] "JBHE Chronology of Major Landmarks in the Progress of African Americans in Higher Education," *The Journal of Blacks in Higher Education*, http://www.jbhe.com/features/53_blackhistory_timeline.html, c.2006, accessed Dec. 7, 2012.

[7] "Memorandum on a recent incident which (words unclear) fundamental considerations in regard to race relations at Earlham," date illegible, found in the archives of Earlham College, Richmond, Indiana.

[8] From a letter dated December 7, 1943, found in the archives of Earlham College, Richmond, Indiana.

[9] From a letter sent by Lilith Farlow, December 19, 1943, found in the archives of Earlham College, Richmond, Indiana.

[10] Robert S. Lynd and Helen Merrell Lynd, *Middletown* (New York: Harcourt, Brace and Company, 1929).

[11] Lynd and Lynd, *Middletown*, 483.

[12] Robert S. and Helen Merrell Lynd, *Middletown in Transition.* (New York: Harcourt, Brace and Company, 1937).

[13] Lynd and Lynd, *Middletown in Transition,* 465.

[14] Lynd and Lynd, *Middletown in Transition,* 463.

[15] Lynd and Lynd, *Middletown in Transition,* 463.

[16] Lynd and Lynd, *Middletown,* 483.

[17] Robert S. Lynd and Helen Merrell Lynd, *Middletown in Transition* (New York: Harcourt, Brace, and Company, 1937), 411.

[18] Blee, 86.

[19] Blee, 134.

[20] Jacqueline Battalora, *Toward a Critical White Racial Ethics: Constructions of Whiteness in Antimescegenation Law*, Ph.D. dissertation, Garrett Evangelical Theological Seminary, Evanston, IL, 1999.

[21] Battalora, 53.

[22] Ernest Porterfield, *Black and White Mixed Marriages* (Chicago:Nelson-Hall,1978), 9-10.

[23] Delany, Sarah and A. Elizabeth, *Having Our Say: The Delany Sisters' First Hundred Years* (New York: Kodansha International,1993).

[24] Keith Buckley, Assistant Director for Public Services, Indiana University Maurer School of Law, email, Dec. 14, 2012.

[25] Brownfeld, Allan, "Mixed Marriage and the Supreme Court," in Clotye M. Larsson, ed., *Marriage Across the Color Line* (Chicago: Johnson Publishing, 1965).

[26] Battalora, 167.

[27] Battalora, 169.

[28] Jeffrey S. Passel, Wendy Wang and Paul Taylor, "Marrying Out," Pew Research Center Publications, June 4, 2010, http://pewresearch.org/pubs/1616/american-marriage-interracial-interethnic

[29] Buckley, email.

[30] The account of Daniel's union days is of course from his point of view, with additional information from Carl Henderson and *The Palladium Item*, Richmond's newspaper.

[31] Blee, 87.

[32] Joel Williamson, *New People: miscegenation and mulattos in the United States* (New York: Free Press, 1980), 73.

[33] Williamson, 98.

[34] Battalora, 162.

[35] Susan Saulny, "Census Data Presents Rise in Multiracial Population of Youths," *The New York Times*, March 24, 2011, http://www.nytimes.com/2011/03/25/us/25race.html?_r=0.

Made in the USA
Columbia, SC
05 February 2018